RECOLLECTIONS OF AN EVANGELIST

RECOLLECTIONS

of an

EVANGELIST

or,

INCIDENTS

CONNECTED WITH

VILLAGE MINISTRY

by

ROBERT GRIBBLE

Missionary in rural Britain, 1815-1847

"Unto me who am less than the least of all saints is this grace given, that I should preach among the Gentiles, the unsearchable riches of Christ."—Ephesians 3:8

SCRIPTURE TESTIMONY EDITION

WALKING TOGETHER PRESS

ESTES PARK · JENTA MANGORO

© 2023 Walking Together Press

Published in 2023 by
Walking Together Press
Estes Park, Colorado USA
Jenta Mangoro, Jos, Plateau Nigeria
https://walkingtogether.press

ISBN: 978-1-961568-20-4

Recollections of an Evangelist is in the public domain
Originally published in 1858 by W. Yapp, London
Text from the 1858 edition

Scripture Testimony Index content © 2023 Walking Together Press, all rights reserved

Cover design by D. Thaine Norris
Typeset in Adobe Garamond Pro by J. Thaine Norris

1

.

ABOUT THE SCRIPTURE TESTIMONY EDITION

Robert Gribble was a Spirit-led evangelist in rural Britain in the early to mid 1800s, an area which—in spite of the presence of the established church—was faithless, ignorant of the Gospel, and often hostile to it. Unlike many who sought to evangelize the unreached, Mr. Gribble was not called to some distant overseas mission, but simply to the next village over. Starting by asking two simple, sincere questions of God, Gribble received the call to ministry and then started a Sunday School, which bore much fruit. Every few years the Holy Spirit led Mr. Gribble to settle in a new village, where he would begin the process over again of being a good neighbor, meeting in homes, preaching on the farms, and thereby introducing scores of people to Jesus. In his forty-two years of ministry, he encountered pervasive human depravity, but also miraculous cases of conversion, intervention, and transformation; for nothing is impossible for God.

This collection of simple testimonies shows the timeless, changeless leading and faithfulness of God. The text of the 1858 book has been typeset and repaired in order to rescue the reader from scanning errors, inkblots, and ponderous early nineteenth century scripture formatting. (such as, Ps. CXXXIV. 3., Jno. III. 16., &c.)

Data science reveals trends and patterns in information. The *Scripture Testimony Index* is an extensive research project using artificial intelligence and data science to develop a New-Testament-driven subject index across a large body of missionary biographies and personal narratives. As the story enthusiasts at Walking Together Press study these books programmatically; beautiful, bright threads emerge—threads of prayer, provision, deliverance, specific leading, healing, transformation, revival, and miraculous conversion. The end result is an index of thousands of short story excerpts organized by subject and Bible verse that empirically demonstrate the truth of the Scriptures, and which is freely available on our website at https://walkingtogether.life. Another result of this research was the discovery of dozens of great books that are long out of print and in danger of being forgotten. The *Scripture Testimony Collection* is a set of such books that we enthusiastically recommend, to the degree that we are making the effort to republish them.

Walking Together Press has enhanced this classic title, *Recollections of an Evangelist,* by adding twenty-eight *Scripture Testimony* boxes in the text identifying Biblical topics and verses that are demonstrated by a specific portion of the narrative. An extensive *Scripture Testimony Index* has been added at the end containing short summaries of how each Scriptural topic is illustrated, making it easier to locate specific stories.

PREFACE

THIS little book has not been written to please any particular class of persons. The chief aim of the Author has been usefulness. In this brief account of forty-two years' labour in the Gospel, he has preferred simplicity and truth to fine language and artificial colouring. He doubts not that many dear people of God will find some refreshment in the perusal of these pages, and he confidently hopes that they may also be used by the Lord for blessing to some who have hitherto been strangers to His grace and love. Should this happily be the case, his highest wishes will be gratified, and the glory shall be given to Him to whom alone it is due.

The "Appendix" contains a few extracts from the writer's journal, added at the suggestion of friends, who considered that some account of the way in which the Lord has sustained him during the last twenty-five years, might form a suitable conclusion to the book. These might have been greatly enlarged, but for a strong desire to keep the size of the volume within moderate limits. Enough however has been inserted to show the providential care of an Heavenly Father who delights to help those who trust in Him, and who, if able to raise such weak instruments in bringing sinners to Himself, can surely provide for His servant's daily need.

—Robert Gribble

CONTENTS

RECOLLECTIONS OF AN EVANGELIST

CHAPTER I

THE FIRST STEP

"Who hath despised the day of small
things?"— Zechariah 4:10

WHEN the Lord first made known His precious salvation
to my own soul, the prevailing thought of my mind
was, "how can I be useful to the souls of others?" I was
continually inquiring, "Lord, what wilt Thou have me to do?" This
desire if sincere and earnest, is never, I believe, disappointed; and it
may be instructive to observe the way in which, in my case, the Lord
was pleased to fulfil it. It occurred to me that my service as a teacher
in the Sunday school of my native town would not be much missed,
while it might be very useful in some of the neighbouring villages.
At that period, 1815, a *village* Sunday school was a new thing in
that part of the country; but the result of this first thought was the
establishment of several within the space of one year, through my
own personal exertions and the help of others who were stirred up
to follow my example, so that nearly three hundred children were
soon brought under religious instruction. The school which was more
especially under my own superintendence was at St. John's Chapel,
three miles from the town of Barnstaple; and on my suggesting to a
minister who was there on a visit, that the people of the village might
be glad to hear a gospel sermon, he willingly consented to preach to

them before his departure. The character of the whole agricultural population in that neighbourhood at this period was that of gross darkness. In a district nearly twenty miles in length there was scarcely any gospel ministry, nor did I know or hear of a single family—one only excepted—where the truth was known or valued. I remember to have heard about that time that some ignorant persons were in the habit of preserving the clothes in which they were married, from an impression that they could not go worthily to the Lord's table without "a wedding garment." Equally ignorant was an old man who told me he was now sure the Bible was true, for his master had lately bought a threshing machine, and it was prophecied that there should be "a new sharp threshing instrument having teeth..." Isaiah 41:15. I have reason to believe that some occasional representations of the spiritual darkness of North Devon at this period, led to the first thought of a Home Missionary Society.

A considerable crowd assembled within and around the cottage where the gospel was first preached in November 1815, and its results were interesting and important, far beyond any previous anticipation. A cry for the gospel was soon heard from these ignorant villagers, and it was responded to on some succeeding week evenings. This, however, did not satisfy, and I was earnestly intreated to provide a Sunday evening service also. But there was no one to undertake this. My heart yearned over the poor villagers, and I longed to send them the bread of life. At length I offered to *read* a sermon to them, and this was gladly accepted; and for a few weeks I read one of Burder's Village Sermons to a crowded congregation of rustic hearers. This was my *first step* in service for the Lord in the gospel. Up to this time I do not remember to have had a single thought of ministry, nor did I consider myself at all qualified for such a work, but I was now drawn into it as by necessity for the sake of others; and, as I *then* thought, merely to supply the present need. "But *my* thoughts are not *your* thoughts, saith the Lord;" and His word to me—although at that time I knew it not—was, "Arise and preach the preaching that I bid thee." Jonah 3:2

I was soon tired of *reading a printed sermon* and began to write one, and was gradually led from step to step until within less than twelve months I usually preached without notes.

I have stated thus much to show how one who, like myself, had received no preparatory instruction for ministry, was led to engage in a work so solemn and responsible; and that at a period, when both by Dissenters and Episcopalians, a certain measure of educational training either in some college or academy, was considered almost indispensable. I was fully aware of this, but was gradually led onwards, impelled by an agency I could not resist.

SCRIPTURE TESTIMONY
Holy Spirit directs believers in ministry
MATTHEW 10:19-20 · ACTS 8:29 · ACTS 13:2 · ACTS 15:28 · ACTS 16:6-10 · ACTS 20:22 · ROMANS 8:14

Within a few months of my first effort to preach some farmers living at Hiscot, another village of the some large parish— Tawstock, requested me to come and minister to them also; and I consented to go there in the morning, so that my time on the Lord's day became fully occupied.

The instruction at the Sunday school was attended with much blessing. About ninety children were collected in a village which contained but twelve or fourteen houses, and several were afterwards converted; two of the earliest scholars have for many years been engaged in the ministry of the gospel.

I know not whether it may have arisen from the way in which I was first called to the work, or from my natural fondness for rural scenes and employments, that my heart has always been especially alive to *village* ministry, and my whole service, with very few exceptions, has been amongst the poorest classes of agriculturists, with whom I have had seasons of joy and blessing to which I shall soon allude.

CHAPTER II

THE FIRST FRUITS OF THE GOSPEL

"Not by might nor by power, but by my spirit
saith the Lord of Hosts."—Zechariah 4:6

WITHIN two years from the preaching of the first
sermon, a chapel had been erected at East Coombe,
(not far from St. Johns Chapel), to accommodate one
hundred and fifty hearers. Many who have long since departed to
be with Christ, were first awakened to a sense of their lost condition and led to Jesus, through the Lord's blessing on the ministry
in that chapel and in the cottage used previous to its erection. If
this had not been the case I should probably have doubted my
call to such a work, but the Lord, in his rich grace, was pleased to
grant me this token of His approval from the very beginning of
my service for Him.

One of the first conver-
sions was that of *blind George,*
an aged man who was also
nearly deaf, so that he could
never hear an address from a
pulpit, but what he *had* heard

SCRIPTURE TESTIMONY
Giving all one has to live on, *and trusting God for provision*
MARK 12:41-44 · LUKE 21:1-4

while sitting near the table in the cottage, had led him to the Lamb
of God; and having found peace through His blood he continued

for some years to adorn the gospel, until gathered as a shock of com fully ripe into the heavenly garner. One or two simple anecdotes of this dear saint are worthy of record. His parish allowance was eighteenpence a week, and of this small pittance one halfpenny was brought every Lord's day to the chapel for missionary purposes. On one occasion he brought *twopence,* and on being asked the reason, he replied, "The Lord has been very good to me this week." I afterwards learned that some one had given him sixpence, and of this, to him, large bounty one-fourth was devoted to the Lord's service. May the bright example of this poor man be made a touchstone to the consciences of all who love the Saviour, and especially of those who are rich in this world. The mites of the poor widow were observed, and her liberality applauded, because she had done what she could.

George loved to be alone in the chapel on Lord's day for some time previous to the commencement of the service, contrary to the practice of many who are habitually late in their attendance. On one of these occasions I asked him what he was thinking about. He said about heaven, where he did not expect a high place; it would be enough for him to be within the gates, and added—

> "Then I shall sing as loud as they
> Who shine afar in bright array."

He afterwards said—

> "Then shall I see, and hear, and know
> All I desired and wished below."

"The Lord can restore all my faculties, sir."

Another early conversion was that of *old Johanna,* who was for some time deterred from going to the chapel, feeling that if she once did this she should never be able to remain away afterwards. Her prognostication was strictly true. She could not resist the inclination to go *once,* and never afterwards wished to absent herself. She became a devoted Christian, and for some years after I preached in her humble dwelling.

Another interesting conversion occurred on the first Lord's day 1820, when the wife of a farmer, who was anxious to hear the New Year's Sermon, came a distance of four miles riding behind her husband on horseback, but found, to her great disappointment, that it was not to be preached until the evening. But her anxiety to hear it was such that her husband was induced to go with her again in the evening, when the word from Isaiah 61:1-2 was used by the Lord for her conversion. This dear woman had afterwards the joy of seeing four of her children brought to a saving knowledge of the truth. One of them, a son, became a devoted, faithful, and greatly honoured servant of the Lord, and much used for the promotion of His glory by preaching the gospel.

It was not to be expected that the god of this world would quietly suffer his dominions to be thus invaded. While the common people, as in days of old, heard the gospel gladly, others were endeavouring by persecution and ridicule to hinder it, but in vain, A neighbouring farmer predicted that the newly-erected chapel would, in a few years, be used as a barn; but after a period of forty years the tidings of salvation are still heard within its walls, while he has long since been called to his account.

Within a mile of the chapel were the residences of two gentlemen of high position, claiming remote and even royal ancestry; both were magistrates, and nearly related, being different branches of the same family. One of them—to his honour be it recorded —never interfered in any way to hinder the gospel, even when ministered almost close to the precincts of his noble mansion; and his example was followed by all the members of his large establishment. By the other we were greatly opposed, and various unworthy means were used to prevent the spread of the new doctrine. Children were met on their way to the Sunday school and driven back; the poor were threatened with the loss of their parish pay if they came to the chapel; the churchwardens were ordered to go and report the persons who attended; and it was said from the pulpit that those who did so endangered their salvation. The Lord's hand was, however, especially seen in His not permitting the other gentleman alluded to to countenance the opposition of his near relative whose influence was comparatively small, while he was himself proprietor of half the extensive parish; and his influence, if exerted against us, would in all probability have caused the work to cease. This, however, could not be, seeing it was the Lord's purpose to bring some members of each of these two families to the knowledge of Himself.

CHAPTER III

THE POWER OF THE WORD OF GOD

"Our gospel came not unto you in word only,
but also in power and in the Holy Ghost, and
in much assurance."—1 Thessalonians 1:5

ABOUT two miles from the chapel was a farm-house which I was accustomed to visit, and sometimes tarried there the night. Part of the household consisted of several men servants and apprentices[1] whose apartment lay above that in which I usually slept, and I was repeatedly much interested by hearing the voice of some one evidently engaged in prayer. I found, on inquiry, that one of the apprentices often prayed with his fellow servants when they retired to rest. This somewhat surprised me having never beheld any marks of seriousness in his general conduct. He possessed, however, great fluency of speech, which

SCRIPTURE TESTIMONY
Scriptures essential for knowing and loving God
2 TIMOTHY 3:14-17
· HEBREWS 4:12

---

1 The children of the poor were commonly bound as apprentices to farmers and others by the overseers of the parish, from the age of eight or nine years until they were twenty-one, the master or mistress providing their whole maintenance but paying no wages.

together with a good memory enabled him to pray like an experienced Christian. He became proud of his ability, and, like the pharisees of old, prayed to be heard and seen of men. Matthew 6:5, and 23:14. On becoming of age he quitted the farm and fell into temptation, the results of which made manifest his true character. Yet he still attended on the ministry of the gospel, keeping up the form of godliness on the Lord's day; but ere long his pharisaic pride and deceit were broken down by the almighty power of divine grace, and he was made to feel himself a poor lost sinner. The immediate cause of his conversion was simply the word of God, according to that scripture, "being born again not of corruptible seed, but incorruptible *by the word of God.*" 1 Peter 1:23. The text of the sermon 1 Corinthians 3:11 was fastened by the Spirit of God on his conscience, and that was sufficient. Of the sermon itself he remembered nothing, but he could not forget the words, *"Other foundation can no man lay than that is laid, which is Jesus Christ."* To him this word was "quick and powerful, sharper than any two-edged sword." Hebrews, 4:12. It discerned the secret thoughts of his heart, tore away the flimsy veil of his self-righteousness, and led him at once to Jesus, "who of God is made unto us wisdom and righteousness, and sanctification, and redemption; that according as it is written, He that glorieth, let him glory in the Lord," 1 Corinthians 1:30-31.

From this time the simple truth of the Bible, called by the apostle "the sincere milk of the word," 1 Peter 2:2, was that in which he especially delighted, and by this his soul was daily fed and nourished. He was thus prepared for the service of God in the gospel, into which he was gradually led, for which he had also been peculiarly trained by the experience of his own heart, and the power of God through the word. Though still employed in daily labour the character of his ministry was considered by experienced believers to be truly edifying. His service was constant, and he was accustomed to go a long distance from his home on the Lord's day. At length he was led to a village fifteen miles off where he laboured with much blessing to many; and he became so attached to this field of service, that for a long time he walked there every Lord's day, being altogether a journey of thirty miles. Yet I have heard his wife remark that he never spoke of his journey with anxiety before he left home, or complained of weariness after his return. A farmer of that neighbourhood much valued his labours and offered him constant employment if he would remove. This would have saved him much labour but he was unwilling to accept it until he had a confident persuasion that it was according to the Lord's will. He knew that the "steps of a good man are ordered by the Lord," and that it is written "commit thy way unto the Lord; trust also in Him; and He shall bring it to pass." Psalm 37:5. Happy would it be if the people of God were always anxious to know the mind of their Heavenly Father, and if in all cases they sought His guidance; for has He not promised to lead us in the way in which we should go? It was two years before he took the step which he considered so important; and during the whole of that time he continued his journey on the Lord's day, patiently seeking guidance respecting his future path. Such disinterested service for God, accompanied with much self-denial, and seeking no earthly reward, is but too rarely witnessed in these days of weakness. It is comparatively unknown to men, but will meet its due recompense in the day when "every man's work shall be made manifest." 1 Corinthians 3:18.

Through an accident which occurred in his daily labour, he was at length unfitted for manual employment; but he is still living, and though advanced in years continues to labour in the work of the Lord, "bringing forth fruit in old age, to show that the Lord is upright, and that there is no unrighteousness in Him," Psalm 92:15.

CHAPTER IV

THE WAGGONER

"My word shall not return unto me void, but it shall accomplish that which I please,"—Isaiah 55:11

A POOR man, of quiet and sober habits, was one evening returning from his labour when he suddenly became thoughtful; and standing still in the road

SCRIPTURE TESTIMONY
A person God has prepared to hear the Gospel
MATTHEW 10:13 · LUKE 10:6

he was led to pray that if he was ignorant of anything needful to his salvation the Lord would reveal it to him. This was the first dawn of light on his hitherto dark mind, preparatory to the more distinct work of the Holy Spirit in convincing him of sin and directing him to the Lamb of God as the one atoning sacrifice. He had not as yet attended the preaching of the gospel, though he had doubtless heard of its effects, and might possibly have seen the change wrought in some of his neighbours by its almighty power. Richard, was the waggoner in the establishment of the gentleman whose active persecution of the gospel has been already noticed; who was thus taught that while he might endeavour to keep his dependents from hearing the truth, he could not prevent its influence from reaching their hearts. He who sent His Son to bring the tidings of salvation

to a ruined world hath declared, "I will work, and who shall let it."
Isaiah 43:18. All the counsels of His will must therefore be fulfilled,
in spite of the enmity of Satan and the opposition of men. This poor
man was little aware of the result of his simple but sincere prayer,
both to his own soul and the souls of others. Coming soon after to
the chapel it was not long before his petition was answered, and he
was made happy in the knowledge which he was already prepared
to receive. He soon became a living witness to the truth, and gave
ample evidence that he was not ashamed of the gospel. I doubt not
but his conversation with those with whom he associated in the
stable related to that which the Lord had done for his soul, Psalm
66:16; and we may judge that his testimony was not in vain, as one
of the grooms was soon afterwards converted and became a decided
follower of Christ. The next trophy of divine grace in this family
was the lady's-maid, who has now for many years been the wife of a
faithful minister of Christ; the latter having received his first religious
impressions in our Sunday school. This was followed some time
after by the conversion of her young mistress, who was enabled to
exhibit much boldness in the faith of Christ. It may truly be said of
this young lady that she denied herself, and took up her cross and
followed Him. It was her lot to encounter much persecution and
reproach, which she cheerfully bore for His name's sake. Her desire
to attend the ministry of the gospel was such, that she frequently
had the courage to go to the despised chapel notwithstanding the
opposition of parents and friends. She knew the love of Him who
hath said, "if any man love father or mother more than me, he is not
worthy of me." One of her near relations, a lady in another branch
of the same family, subsequently received the truth, whose son also
was converted, and has long been labouring as a clergyman in a wide
field of service as a faithful servant of the Lord Jesus.

In this silent manner did the truth find its way from the cottage
to the mansion, according to His purpose, "who worketh after the
counsel of His own will." Ephesians 1:11. The light which began
to shine in a corner of a parish many miles in extent had now

enlightened many hearts; and although a great number had not heard the gospel, yet its influence was felt, and its effects were seen, and a spirit of inquiry was excited. The people generally were not now satisfied with a ministry which merely inculcated moral duties and self-righteous formality, and left its hearers in total ignorance of the way of salvation, and to their great joy they were at length gratified by hearing the free offers of the gospel of the grace of God in the parish church. The whole patronage of the parish being in the hands of the family alluded to, and the incumbent being advanced in years, a curate was procured, and the gospel was preached in its fulness within the walls of the ancient edifice—where tattered banners hung over the proud monuments of the departed dead.

Another important event soon followed. It was thought desirable to provide suitable instruction for the children of the poor; and a convenient school-room was erected in a lovely and romantic spot, where all who desired it might send their children for moral and religious instruction. A godly schoolmaster, whose heart was in the work, was also obtained, who laboured earnestly to promote their welfare by instilling into their young minds the truth which alone could make them wise unto salvation.

It is instructive to observe, that what has been related in this chapter was the result of the conversion of the poor waggoner, who was one that feared God among many. I once saw him when under the influence of painful disease, and for some days he was quite blind; while conversing with him about his trial, he observed that he could never pray for the removal of any affliction, but only that it might be sanctified. Surely we cannot contemplate this work of the Lord without thankfulness and praise to Him, who in fulfilling the purposes of His mercy chooses the foolish things of the world to confound the wise, and the weak things of the world, to confound the things which are mighty, and base things of the world, and things that are despised, yea, and things which are not, to bring to nought things that are, that no flesh should glory in His presence. 1 Corinthians 1:27-29.

CHAPTER V

THE SHOEMAKER

"If any man be in Christ, he is a new creature." —2 Corinthians 5:17

A T the request of a Christian friend I sometimes went to preach at Chawleigh, a village twenty miles distant, where the Lord had gathered some souls to Himself by the preaching of the gospel; and my occasional labours there were not permitted to be altogether in vain. Among other

interesting circumstances was the following remarkable conversion. It was late in November when I was engaged to preach at the early hour of nine o'clock on the Lord's day morning, being expected elsewhere at eleven. The wife of a shoemaker residing in the village, and who had been convinced of sin, was anxious to bring her husband under the sound of the gospel, and the coming of a stranger was considered a fit opportunity to urge him to go with her. Like Felix, however, he made many excuses. It was not "a convenient season," Acts 24:25, for "he had to take to his customers the shoes made during the previous week." But the Lord's purposes of mercy respecting him were not to be set aside, and it may truly he said of him that he was "made willing in the day of his power." As the hour for meeting was so early, he was at length prevailed on to go, saying he might perhaps have time to take the shoes after the service. The word preached was from the portion of scripture at the head of this chapter, 2 Corinthians 5:17: "if any man be in Christ he is a new creature and this truth has perhaps seldom been more strikingly confirmed than on this occasion. I do not remember ever to have ministered with more conscious power in my own soul than while delivering the message of the gospel at this early hour on a wintry morning; nor have I ever seen an individual so deeply affected as was this poor shoemaker while listening to its voice. From that hour he became "a new creature," indeed, a living testimony to the truth he had just heard, and the whole course of his future life gave ample proof that "old things had passed away, and all things become new." It is scarcely necessary to add that the shoes remained, in his house till the Lord's day was past, nor was the old practice ever afterwards renewed.

For some time after his faith was tried by decline in business. Some of his customers showing their dislike of his new doctrine by withdrawing their custom from him. But who ever trusted in the Lord and was confounded? He was enabled to go on, seeking to conduct his business in the fear of the Lord, and was at length so prospered that he told me it was nearly doubled, and required him to employ *two* extra hands. This was a new era in his life, and at no distant period he began to preach the gospel to others. He subsequently left his business and took a small farm in a neighbourhood where his labours in the Lord's service were very abundant.

Another circumstance, equally important in its results, arose out of my occasional labours at Chawleigh. Previous to my first visit I had been much interested in the account which I had heard of a poor believer in that place, and became anxious to know him. Those who have had much intercourse with poor saints, of warm hearts and spiritual minds, well know that if these qualities are combined with simplicity of character the countenance will sometimes so shine as to indicate the joy that dwells within, and it was truly thus with the dear brother alluded to. When I saw him enter the little chapel I immediately concluded that that man with the smock frock and the bright happy countenance was the individual I had heard of; and I was not mistaken, for when, after the close of the service, I said to him, "is your name S——?" he replied, "yes, bless the Lord," and the acquaintance which commenced at that moment was destined by Him who orders the paths of our feet to lead to results which altered the whole course of his future life, and brought much glory to God, as will soon be related. This dear Christian had hitherto acquired but little knowledge of divine truth. He knew Jesus, "whom to know is eternal life," John 17:3, and much loved Him; but he knew not as yet the blessed liberty with which He makes His people free. It was, however, the Lord's good pleasure to make known to him this blessing soon after our first acquaintance. Love and zeal were happily combined in his character, and this was manifested by his earnest desire to commend to others the truth which had been so blessed to his own soul. He was then in the employ of the late Earl of Portsmouth; but the place of his work being three miles distant he became dissatisfied, fearing his health and strength would suffer from so much extra exertion, in addition to his daily labour. He was on this account very anxious to obtain more easy employment, of which more will be said in another chapter.

CHAPTER VI

THE MIDNIGHT VISIT

"Behold how good and how pleasant it is for brethren
to dwell together in unity."—Psalm 133:1

IT was not long after the waggoner's (Richard's) conversion, when
he informed me he was soon to go a journey of forty miles with
his master's waggon. Being in the warmth of his first love he
was much concerned about this; for although he had always been a
comparatively moral man he was not averse to the vain conversation
of those who assembled at the ale house, which he now dreaded and
hated. He was grieved to think he should have no opportunity of
enjoying Christian communion by the way. It happened that the
village mentioned in the last chapter lay about half way on the road
to the place where he was sent, and he heard with much pleasure
that a Christian brother who lived there would be glad to see him.
He left home with high expectations of seeing this dear friend, but
was disappointed at finding that he was always from home in the
day time. To his great joy, he was soon after ordered to go to the
same place a second time, and he now resolved, if possible, to see
him. As he went he called and told S——'s wife he should not fail
to stop on his return, though it might possibly be very late. Being
detained longer than he expected it was past midnight when he again
arrived at the village, and on knocking at the door he was surprised

at the speed with which his hitherto unknown friend had put on his clothes and come down to open it. He was received with that warmth of true Christian affection which those alone who love the Saviour can exhibit or fully understand.

The first act of the kind host was to go to the inn and care for his friend's horses; after which he returned to provide the best refreshment his humble cottage afforded. The remainder of the night was spent in happy fellowship and prayer, for to them its hours were too precious to be wasted in sleep, though the labour of the preceding day might seem to have required it. The nightly revels which are sometimes held in the halls and palaces of the great are blazoned forth in the annals of this world. The meeting of these poor men may boast of a higher record, being inscribed in that book of remembrance which is ever before Him who hearkens to the converse of those who fear Him and call upon His name Malachi 3:16; whom He will also own as His jewels in the day of His appearing— the day when the kings and mighty ones of the earth, who are not born of God, will call on the mountains and rocks to fall on them, and hide them from the wrath of the Lamb. Revelation 6:16.

When the morning began to dawn, it was seen by the countenance of his host that the time had arrived for him to depart to his daily labour; and after commending each other to the care of their Father in heaven, the two brethren proceeded to their respective employments. Both of them afterwards told me that this was one of the happiest seasons they had ever enjoyed.

Truly "love is of God, and he that loveth not knoweth not God, for God is love;" "and this commandment have we from Him, that he who loveth God love his brother also." 1 John 4:7-8,21. These poor men had but lately known the love which the Lord had towards them; and they knew but little—perhaps nothing— about creeds and systems; but they had been taught of God to love one another, and if their attainments in the divine life are judged by this standard they had far outstripped some who are much older in the school of Christ, in these days when the love of many has waxed cold.

To those who *know not* the love of Jesus, the history of this night-scene, which requires an abler pen than mine to do it justice, may perhaps excite a smile, as being exceedingly strange, if not enthusiastic, or both. They are able to understand how many can spend a whole night in busy revelry, and join the giddy dance; others listening to the unchaste song, or draining the intoxicating bowl; for in these so-called enjoyments there is that which meets the perpetual inquiry, "who will show us any good?" and these pleasures may tend *for a time* "to silence the voice of conscience;" but that two poor men, who never saw each other before, alike ignorant and unlearned, should deny themselves the enjoyment of needful repose to spend the night in prayer and talking about the Bible, is beyond their comprehension. This will not, however, surprise any who know and value the word of God, for that blessed book declares that "the natural man receiveth not the things of the spirit of God, for they are foolishness unto him, *neither can he know them,* because they are spiritually discerned." 1 Corinthians 2:14.

Those, however, who have been taught of God, will peruse this incident with very different feelings; and some may perhaps he reminded of those early days of the church recorded in Acts 2:44, "when all that believed had all things common," and "great grace was upon them all" Acts 4:83; and they may be led to pray that the love so sweetly exhibited in this humble cottage may be more frequently seen in the busy town and the crowded city.

> "O, 'tis sweet each other aiding,
>   In companionship to move;
> One desire each heart pervading,
>   One our Lord, our faith, our love.
> Sweet when each can bend, imploring,
>   Soothing for his brother's pain,
> And the stumbling soul restoring,
>   Cheer him to the race again."

CHAPTER VII

MAN'S WILL AND GOD'S PURPOSE

"A man's heart deviseth his way; but the Lord
directeth his steps."—Proverbs 16:9

THE future history of S—— is interesting and instructive,
and so connected with the Lord's work that some account of
it is necessary. Owing to his discontent with his daily labour
from its being so far from his home, he resolved at last to go to a lace
factory in a town some miles distant. I endeavoured to dissuade him
from this, feeling he was likely to be useful in his present position,
and placed Lot's history before him, fearing that he might be actuated
by some latent feeling of covetousness. But finding that all counsel
was unavailing, I suggested his coming to Barnstaple, where there was
also a factory in which I doubted not he might procure employment.
He willingly assented to this, and in a short time became my near
neighbour, always accompanying me in my journeys on the Lord's
day, when our communion by the way was oftentimes very sweet. It
is usual in these factories to employ new hands, during the first year,
as labourers; after which they have a loom, when their wages are
increased, varying according to their ability. S—— anxiously anticipated the close of this period of probation, hoping to share the advantages which would enable him to maintain his family with some
degree of comfort. This hope, however, was not to be realised: he had

25

quitted his former employment according to *his own will*, not knowing that *the Lord* had *His purpose* to accomplish by it. Just at the time when he expected the fulfilment of his hopes, the proprietor of the factory resolved to reduce the number of his workmen, and the young-est hands, of which S—— was one, were suddenly discharged. His prospects being thus blasted, his disappointment was deep and severe. He soon came to me with his tale of sorrow, not knowing what to do, but feeling very unwilling to return to his former place. I sought to comfort him by saying that if he was willing again to labour as an agriculturist he might perhaps obtain it from a Christian farmer living two miles from the chapel, to whom he was well known from their frequently meeting there. The offer was gladly accepted, and he was soon settled there.[2]

SCRIPTURE TESTIMONY
All great movements of God are birthed in prayer
ACTS 1:14 · ACTS 4:31

There were not any believ-ing men at that time in the village, which lay close to the farm, except the farmer and one of his workmen, whose conversion is noticed in Chapter III; but as soon as S—— was settled in his cottage he determined to hold a prayer-meeting. He was told it would be of no use and no one would attend. S——, however, was not more conspicuous for love and zeal than for decision and firmness; and his immediate reply was, "then I will hold one by myself." The matter was of course settled, and it was immediately determined that his cottage should be used for a prayer-meeting at nine o'clock on Sunday mornings.

To the surprise of many this meeting was well attended from the beginning; and to the joy also of some it was often found to be

---

2   This was the farm alluded to in Chapter III, and the farmer was one of the only Christian family (mentioned in Chapter I), in a large district; and it will be interesting to many to know that the Lord's work in that family resulted from the conversation of that faithful servant of God the late Richard Knill, during his occasional visits there which led to the conversion of this farmer, his brother, and four sisters. The writer's union with one of the latter in 1815, first led his thoughts to that neighbourhood as a fit place of service for the Lord.

a season of refreshment through the manifest tokens of the Lord's presence; proving that He is not confined to any building whatever, but may always be expected where but two or three meet in the name of Jesus. The blessing which this dear servant of God so earnestly desired to realise was not witheld. Some souls were born to God in his house, two of which I distinctly remember. The first was the wife of the farmer of whom he rented his cottage. The next was a pedlar living in a village half a mile off. He had, on a Lord's day morning, quarrelled with his wife for refusing to open their shop. She had recently been convinced of sin, and wished to decline all business on the Lord's day; but as there was a rival shop near their own, the poor husband feared the loss of their custom if theirs was closed. Strange to relate he went to the prayer-meeting when the quarrel was ended, perhaps from some conviction that he had acted wrong and hoping to make some atonement; but he was unconsciously directed there by One whom as yet he knew not, and who had purposes of mercy respecting him. I was not present on that occasion, but a young man came to unite in their worship and on his arrival S—— said he hoped he would "give them a word that morning;" it was replied that as it was simply a prayer-meeting he had no intention to minister; being told, however, that Mr. G—— generally did so, this young Christian, who had but lately begun to speak in the name of the Lord, gave a very short address from the words "behold he prayeth," Acts 9:11. They were sent as an arrow to the poor pedlar's heart, who, on returning home, asked his wife's forgiveness and assured her they should never quarrel about the shop again. Family prayer was commenced in his house the same day, and from that time he and his wife lived happily together walking in the good ways of the Lord. He afterwards became a helper in the ministry of the word.

It was now plainly seen why S—— was permitted to leave his former employment; and he became fully satisfied that his own plans were overruled to fulfil some blessed purpose of the Lord's mercy, and he was abundantly compensated for all his previous disappointment. The prayer-meeting was a means of much blessing in a place where vice and ungodliness were almost proverbial; and it was so well attended that a small chapel was considered needful. This object was so generally approved that it was completed without contracting any debt exactly one year

> **SCRIPTURE TESTIMONY**
>
> *Christian communities growing through fellowship*
>
> ACTS 2:42 · ROMANS 12:13

after S——'s arrival in the village. The gospel preached within its walls has been used for bringing many souls to Christ. It was built to accommodate about one hundred hearers; but the attendance became so numerous that it was found needful to enlarge it about ten years after. I had quitted the neighbourhood some time previous, but was present at its reopening, when my heart was made glad by witnessing the blessed effects of the gospel. The whole character of the village was changed; many stubborn hearts had yielded to the influence of truth, and the number of believers appeared to be larger in proportion to the whole population than in any other village with which I was acquainted.

The Lord had led S—— by a way which he knew not; he had acted with integrity of purpose, and was yet to have the desire of his heart fulfilled. He had been made willing to go back to his former occupation when he plainly discovered the Lord's mind, and his faith and patience having been proved in the place whither, he was sent for much blessing, another sphere of usefulness was now opened for him. A Christian gentleman who had taken a large farm wished to procure a godly man as bailiff to superintend it. His brother, who was then residing among the poor saints, and ministering at the two chapels, recommended S—— as one suited to fill this responsible situation. All the arrangements being soon made, he removed with his new master to a place many miles distant. I once visited him there, and found him in circumstances as comfortable as he could desire. The Lord had blessed him in all things, and he was made to know that "The steps of a good man are ordered by the Lord."—Psalm 37:23. A large room near his cottage had been fitted up for the ministry of the gospel, and the master and servant preached alternately every Lord's day, to their poor neighbours, each in his turn being minister and hearer. Living at a distance I have heard few particulars of him since that time.

I omitted to observe that soon after the erection of the chapel, the waggoner was suddenly dismissed from his employment, after many years of faithful service, without any assigned cause. He then came to reside in the village to which S—— had been so providentially directed, and the two brethren whose first happy meeting at midnight has been already related, and who then resided twenty miles apart, were now brought to the same place, and for many years were near neighbours, the waggoner, now in old age, still remaining there.

> "In faith and love thy course of duty run,
> God nothing does, nor suffers to be done,
> But thou would'st do the same if thou could'st see
> The end of all events as well as HE."

CHAPTER VIII

THE BACKSLIDER

"Thine own wickedness shall correct thee, and thy blackslidings shall reprove thee,"—Jeremiah 2:19

PERHAPS few histories are more instructive to a spiritual mind than those of persons who having known the joy of pardoned sin, and reconciliation with God, through the blood of Jesus, have turned aside from the good ways of the Lord, and brought reproach on His holy name by open sin. The watchful enemy who is the serpent, Genesis 3:1, and the fowler, Psalm 91:3, is constantly laying snares for our feet, and not a few alas! are caught therein. This is abundantly evident to all. The covetousness of Lot, Genesis 13:10; the intemperance of Noah, Genesis 9:21; the adultery of David, 2 Samuel 11; the idolatry of Solomon, 2 Kings 11:4-5; the pride of Hezekiah, 2 Kings, 20:12; the wilful disobedience of Jonah, chapter 1; the self-confidence of Peter, and its fearful results in the denial of his Lord, Matthew 26:33, 72, give us distinct examples of the various ways, by which the children of God are tempted to depart from Him. The principle on which He dealt with backsliding Israel is declared in Psalm 89:30, "If his children forsake my law, and walk not in my judgments; if they break my statutes, and keep not my commandments; then will I visit their transgressions with the rod, and their iniquity with stripes; nevertheless my loving-kindness will

I not utterly take from him, nor suffer my faithfulness to fail," and the Lord acts on the same principle with individual believers now. Those who have much observed the Lord's dealings with His saints for any lengthened period, may have seen many examples of this, and some such will form the subject of the present chapter.

W—— K—— resided in a village where I statedly laboured. It was his usual custom to spend the whole of the Lord's day in bed, only quitting it to come down to his meals and return again. While lying there, it once occurred to him that the scripture declared that the sleeper should come to poverty. Having searched for, and found the text (perhaps Proverbs 20:13) he came to hear the gospel, and was ere long converted. He gave much evidence of true grace, but the whole of his course, with some few exceptions, was like his natural character variable and unsteady. He was kind and generous to an extreme, sometimes giving his last sixpence to a brother whom he knew to be in need; but he had no fixed rule of conduct, being guided by the impulses of a stubborn self-will. Like Reuben, he was unstable as water, and did not excel. Genesis 49:4. He was continually dissatisfied with himself and with others. Within a few years he was at different times a farm labourer, a boatman, a navvie, and a miner. He was conscious that his frequent changes, and his daily intercourse with wicked men, led him into temptation, and candidly confessed his failures; but he gained no benefit from past experience, except when brought into deep trial through his sin and folly. At one time he was accustomed on the market day to act as hostler in the yard of a public house, and was frequently spoken to and shown the sin into which this might lead him, and the inconsistency of such an employment for one who professed the name of Jesus, but he was deaf to reproof, and continued to pursue his own course, till the Lord compelled him by His chastening rod to feel that it was an "evil thing and bitter" to depart from Him. Jeremiah 2:19. The place of temptation was the scene of his chastisement. His leg was broken in that same inn-yard where he had been so faithfully warned not to stay, and he lamented his folly only when it was too late to avoid its consequences.

There was, however, much mercy mingled with the chastening, as it brought him to his right mind. In the hospital his conduct was that of a humbled but consciously pardoned penitent, who could joyfully praise the Lord for all His dealings towards him, and he felt that the affliction was sent in mercy to restore his soul. He continued to run well for some time after his recovery, and occasionally took part in some meetings for social worship. But it was with him as with Lot, who failed to profit by the past and remained in Sodom till a deeper judgment compelled him to flee from it, and leave all the wealth his heart was so set upon to be destroyed. Poor K——'s instability gradually returned, and he again became wavering and dissatisfied. His wife, who at first persecuted him but had now been converted, suffered much from his wayward temper, when she pointed out to him the inconsistency of his conduct. At length he determined to go to America, in spite of the counsel of many Christian friends, who sought to dissuade him feeling assured it would not prosper; but kind counsel and faithful warnings were alike unheeded, and he was ere long to prove that "The backslider in heart shall be filled with his own ways." Proverbs 14:14. His poor wife was very averse to this step, but he resolved to go by himself if she did not accompany him. I met him unexpectedly a short time previous to his departure, and was deeply tried. He was evidently not happy, and seemed to admit that the Lord might in some way visit him with a fresh stroke of His chastening rod. Such is the perverse wilfulness of the flesh, and such will ever be the wretched experience of all who continue to despise the chastening of the Lord, until He says of them as of Ephraim, "he is joined to idols let him alone." Hosea 4:17.

The remainder of his solemn but deeply instructive history is soon told. He had only been a few weeks in America, and was excavating in the city of Toronto, when a large mass of earth fell on him, and instantly deprived him of life. "If we would judge ourselves, we should not be judged; but when we are judged, we are chastened of the Lord, that we should not be condemned with the world." I Corinthians 11:31-32.

A second instance of divine chastening may be noticed in connection with the foregoing. Mary N——— who had for some time borne testimony to the truth through the whole of her Christian profession, became attached to a young man who had sought to win her affections. She knew that even his moral character was not unexceptionable and also that the precepts of the New Testament forbade the union of Christians with the world, 2 Corinthians 6:14, but she was as one bound by a spell which could not be broken. I was not living near her at this time, but once saw her while on a visit to the place, and warned her of her danger in reference to the event which was soon anticipated. She said very little in reply, but evidently acknowledged the truth of all that was said to her. It was not long after when I received a letter from one of the brethren, stating that a special meeting for prayer had been held in reference to the intended marriage of Mary N———, and it had been answered in a way quite unexpected. This meeting was held on a Friday evening, the wedding being expected to take place on the following Monday. But "go to now, ye that say to-day or to-morrow," &c., "whereas ye know not what shall be on the morrow." James 4:14. On the day after that meeting, Mary was suddenly taken ill; when danger was apprehended, a surgeon was sent for, who made some excuse for not coming; and before other help could be obtained, she was no more! Her death was so sudden as to require a coroner's inquest, when the verdict of the jury stated that her death was to be attributed to the want of medical aid.

> "I was a wandering sheep,
>   I did not love the fold;
> I did not love my Shepherd's voice,
>   I would not be control'd;
> I was a wayward child,
>   I did not love my home;
> I did not love my father's voice
>   I loved afar to roam!"—H. BONAR.

CHAPTER IX

GRACEY, THE SCHOOLMISTRESS

"A woman that feareth the Lord, she shall
be praised."—Proverbs 31:30

ABOUT the period of which I am writing, two benevolent Christians passed through Barnstaple, one of whom was the secretary of the Tract Society, and the other was, I believe, active in the formation of the Home Missionary Society, which had its commencement soon after. Their object in this journey was to make enquiry concerning the spiritual destitution of some of the dark parts of that locality, about which I had some conversation with them. Their first stage from Barnstaple lay over a wretched road, through a wild and barren country, which may account for the breaking down of their carriage; this providentially occurred near Paracombe, a small village, surrounded by moors and commons. They found there no public accommodation for travellers in which to tarry the night, but they were hospitably entertained at a farmhouse near the village, when they soon enquired if there was a Sunday school in or near the place. It is probable, however, that even the *name* of a Sunday school had never been heard there until this time; but the farmers wife observed that the village schoolmistress, Grace Jones, was very fond of children, and would probably like to keep one; and at the request of the strangers she was sent for. It being rather late, Gracey—the name by which she was generally known—was in bed; but she joyfully responded to the summons, and soon arose and came to see the travellers, who intended, if possible, to leave early next morning. They were much interested with her appearance and manner, and she was told, to her great joy, that books of different kinds would soon be sent from London to enable her to begin the Sunday school. On the next day, the news spread rapidly through the village that two gentlemen were going to send Gracey a box of books from London, when all who desired it might send their children to the Sunday school. Few, however, believed this. The general opinion of the ignorant villagers was that Gracey would be disappointed, and the gentlemen had made a fool of her. And for a time it seemed as though they had judged rightly, for the hooks were long expected in vain. But after much delay, it was found on enquiry that the vessel by which they had been forwarded had been shipwrecked during her voyage.. A fresh box, however, was soon sent and the school commenced.

Gracey was remarkably gifted by the Lord for this instruction of the young. Her manner was so kind and winning that she always secured their love, while her method of communicating knowledge was peculiarly her own, and excited interest and attention. A word, or even a look, was sufficient to ensure the most perfect discipline; so that in a school of about twenty children the utmost order was always seen. When she sometimes visited me during the vacation, she always gained the affections of my own dear children. I have reason to believe that she was not herself converted when she began the Sunday School; but she was gradually led into the truth while seeking to make it known to others. Her whole heart was in the work. When the village was visited by a flood, her only anxiety during that night was about the box containing the Bible and hymn-books, lest they should be injured; which as she lived at the bottom of the village, and close to the mill, happened to be the case; but on this and many other occasions, the Lord raised up willing helpers to supply what 'was needful for the furtherance of her useful labours.

A small book was published two years ago, entitled "Christ in the Cottage, and Christ in the Mansion."[3] It was written by a clergyman who called on me at Barnstaple, after having in a very accidental way gone to the village where Gracey resided, which was a few miles from Lynton a favourite watering place on the sea coast. His account of a visit to her school is very interesting, and a few extracts will I am sure be acceptable, and tend to confirm my judgment respecting this poor but truly excellent woman.

The account given of Gracey by the landlady of the town is thus graphically described. "I asked, is there a Sunday school in the parish?"—"O yes! there is as many as seventy children, and set up by a poor woman." "What," said I, "a Sunday school of seventy children, and set up by a poor woman!"—"Aye, it's as sure as you stand there, and she's so poor, that sometimes she can't scramble on without parish relief. Sure enough she's a wonderful woman : I never saw the like of her. She knows as much of her Bible as any parson: and you would be surprised to hear how the children of her school answer questions; and they are so pretty behaved too. There are some wild swearing chaps here amongst the men in this place, but they dare na' swear in her presence; and yet she's a poor little woman, and a cripple too."

Describing his visit, he says :—"I entered and found the children ranged around, and Grace the nucleus of the circle. They were reading the history of Joseph. She, a little woman, crippled, raised up on a pair of pattens, to allow full scope for her large black intelligent brilliant eyes, which no nuts or playthings or cake could possibly escape. I retreated into a corner near enough to hear all that passed, and not near enough to disturb the teacher or distract the children. I was quite delighted. Her questions were so apposite, her remarks so enlightened, so practical; her reflections as to the subject-matter before her' so judicious; her manner animated; her heart and tongue in evident coincidence. No wonder that every eye was fixed upon her. The interest expressed in the children's countenances as she

---

3   Published by Groom.

proceeded, told you that they felt there was a reality in what was urged upon them. As the clock struck twelve she waved her hand, and her little children departed."

The remaining extracts are in Gracey's own words. "I was once a worldly woman, blind as to the concerns of my soul, and ignorant of a Saviour. I was always fond of reading, and got my neighbours to subscribe to a circulating library in the next town. So we got novels and such kind of trash, and so it went on for some time. I kept a school for a livelihood, but I did not teach the children the Bible, for I did not understand it myself. However, it came into my mind one day these novels are not quite the thing; I think I will begin to read the Bible; and as I read on I saw it would never do to go to novels again, and I began for the first time to have a real concern about my soul and a real desire to be saved. I had no one to talk to me about these things, but I read in my Bible about Jesus Christ and what he had done to save sinners; and I felt I was a sinner and needed such a Saviour. So the Lord led me to put my trust in Him, and to love Him, and serve Him.

"There are two little girls who were taken to the wake the other day by their parents. These wakes, sir, are dreadful scenes of wickedness. So these dear little creatures got leave to go to a room by themselves; and there they went, and sang their hymns and read their chapters, while their parents were at the wake, till it was time to go home. And, sir, I will tell you another thing, for I see you like to hear about my children.

SCRIPTURE TESTIMONY
Believers are light in the Lord
2 CORINTHIANS 4:6
· EPHESIANS 5:8
The righteous innately have God's heart toward those in need
MATTHEW 25:31-46

"There was a poor wicked woman who lived in a solitary house at the end of the village. She got very ill so that she could hardly help herself. One day a neighbour called on her and found her reading her Bible, and two of my children were sitting in a corner of the room. This neighbour talked to her and the woman seemed quite serious; and instead of blaspheming and cursing, as she always did before, she talked so nicely about the Lord, and about the Saviour, that the neighbour was astonished. 'Well, Jenny,' said she,' who taught you all this?'—'Ah,' said Jenny, 'it is these two little angels,' pointing to the two little girls in the corner of the room, 'they came to me in their play hours, and swept my room, and made everything comfortable for me; and they fetched me water from the well; and then they would sit down and read their testaments to me. And they talked to me about my soul and told me of a Saviour; and if I get to heaven at last it will be owing to these dear little creatures.'"

CHAPTER X

RETROSPECT

"Thou shalt remember all the way which the
Lord thy God led thee these forty years in
the wilderness,"—Deuteronomy 8:2

IN the preceding pages I have related some of the interesting
events connected with the first period of my ministry, a period
of fourteen years. During this time I had been engaged in business, and had prayed much to be freed from its cares, that I might
devote my whole time to the work in which the Lord had granted
me much blessing. My prayer was at length answered, but it was by
a course of trial and discipline which I had little expected. Yet deep
and painful as it was I had cause to bless God for it all, when made
to see that He was thereby fulfilling His own purpose of bringing
many souls to Himself. It was, however, a heavy stroke to be so
suddenly removed from a people so endeared to me in the bonds
of love and Christian fellowship.

But it was no small consolation to me that they were not left
destitute of pastoral oversight and the ministry of the Word, which
need was provided for in a way altogether unsought and unexpected.
Mr. Thomas Pugsley, a gentleman living in the same town, had been
the subject of a remarkable conversion while absent from home,
and on his return gave abundant testimony to the gospel by his

entire separation from those scenes of gaiety in which he had hitherto associated with the first society in the neighbourhood. In whatever company he might be he showed that he was not ashamed of the gospel of Christ, and he soon gave up a very lucrative profession which he thought he could not conscientiously retain. When I was walking with him on one occasion we were met by a gay young clergyman who said to him, "well, P——, what is *your text?*"—"Woe to you lawyers?" His immediate reply was, *"No—my* text is, 'No man that warreth entangleth himself with the affairs of this life, that he may please him who hath chosen him to be a soldier.'" 2 Timothy 2:4. He was greatly interested in the work at Tawstock, and became so attached to the dear saints there that on my leaving the neighbourhood he willingly devoted his time and strength to their service. He built a house in the same locality, and resided there as a faithful pastor until the close of his life about five years afterwards. The hand of the Lord will be seen here by all who are "wise and will *observe* these things." Psalm 107:43. Nor were the dear people left destitute after his removal. Another disinterested servant of God, Charles Shepherd, soon after came among them, and laboured with much blessing for many years. He also is now entered into rest, but through the whole period of forty years since the erection of the chapel at East Coombe, ministry has not failed, nor has the work, to my knowledge, ever been helped by any public society.

When I quitted Barnstaple there were about thirty believers in communion, besides which many had either left the neighbourhood or fallen asleep in Jesus. Much success has since attended the ministry of the word. I was told some time ago that the whole number of those who had at different times been admitted into communion there was more than a hundred and fifty, of whom about one third still remain. I ought to add, that there are now three chapels connected with this work, one having been built at Hiscot by that dear brother Thomas Pugsley after I left.[4]

---

4   This chapel is alluded to in "The Lord's Gracious Dealings with G. Muller," who preached at its opening when two souls were converted.—p. 67

It has been no small comfort to me that the Lord raised up among those whom he had converted during this period, five individuals whom he used in after years in occasional or stated ministry, two of whom were from our Sunday school; and a still more interesting event occurred soon after my removal. This village congregation was to have the privilege and honour of sending an ambassador to the heathen. A young man, who was apprenticed to a neighbouring farmer, was led to attend the weekly prayer meeting and was ere long converted. It is worthy of remark that the individual through whose prayer he was

> ### SCRIPTURE TESTIMONY
>
> *God lifts up the weak,*
> *works through them, thereby*
> *shaming the strong*
>
> 1 CORINTHIANS 1:27 ·
> 1 THESSALONIANS 5:14

first awakened, had never prayed in our meetings up to the time of my leaving, and had often lamented to me his inability. But the Lord delights to exhibit His sovereignty and power by using "the weak things of the world to confound the things that are mighty." The new convert had to endure some persecution from the family with whom he lived and bore it with much cheerfulness, sometimes singing a hymn outside the door when refused admittance on his return from the prayer meeting. He was quite uneducated like almost all of his class, parish apprentices being generally placed out as soon as they were able to do any kind of work, and their mental improvement being seldom thought of. But being taught by the Holy Spirit this dear youth evinced much zeal for the divine glory; he also made much progress in useful knowledge, and soon gave evidence of gift for the Lord's service. About seven or eight years after this he accompanied the late A. N. Groves to India, where he laboured as a faithful missionary. He was removed from a scene of great usefulness a short time ago while in the prime of life, and now rests from his labours, after having won the esteem of many who loved him for his works' sake, and in which the Lord eminently blessed him. The name of George Beer will be familiar to many who read these lines. His widowed partner still remains in India and devotes her time to the instruction of native children.

At the time of my leaving business I was enabled calmly to wait on the Lord in the full confidence that He had purposes of blessing to accomplish by it, and I was not permitted to be anxious about the future. Nor was my faith tried for any lengthened period, since the Lord was pleased in a most remarkable manner to direct my steps to a Home Missionary Station in a distant part of the same county, under the direction of the ministers of the Independent denomination of that district. I was thus called still to labour among the agricultural poor, to whom I have always been particularly attached. As the locality was quite new to me I had no acquaintances there, but I considered it an especial token of the Lord's kindness that on the same day in which I first saw the village where I was about to live, I met on the outside of a stage coach a Christian brother Wm. Hake who resided twelve miles from it; and the acquaintance then commenced soon matured into a friendship which has continued without any diminution to this day. This providential meeting was very important in its results, as being the means of my introduction to many hitherto unknown friends, through whom my knowledge of divine truth, which had hitherto been very limited, was greatly enlarged.

CHAPTER XI

THE HOME MISSIONARY STATION

"Having a form of godliness but denying the power thereof; from such turn away."—2 Timothy 52:5

I entered on the duties of my new sphere of service as a "Home Missionary" with energy and zeal; and longed to behold, as heretofore, the fruit of my labour. But the character of the service was very different. I had hitherto sown the seed of truth where Christ was scarcely named, but here the people had heard the gospel many years, and there were several loose professors around, who had in various ways brought reproach on the name of Christ and occasioned His enemies to blaspheme. My work therefore was arduous and discouraging, and it was more than a year before I had the happiness of knowing that even one soul had been converted to God. But it has since appeared that one especial purpose for which I was sent to that place was to be instructed in many important truths, which were now gradually opened to me. It was at this time I first began to see the necessity of testing all I professed to believe as God's truth, *by God's own word.* This was a new thing to me, having been accustomed—as many I fear still are—to receive what I had been taught, without taking the pains to examine whether it was in accordance with the Scriptures, the only infallible standard of truth. "To the law and to the testimony &c." Isaiah 8:20. I now began to follow the example of the noble Bereans, who "searched the Scriptures daily" Acts 17:11 in obedience to the precept, John 5:39 and was led earnestly to pray for divine light and guidance. I have ever since had cause to be thankful that from this time my chief anxiety was to know the *Lord's* mind concerning His truth which I desired to follow without regarding consequences.

I now began to discover my profound ignorance respecting the prophetic word, and wondered how I could have so long applied to the church those portions which so plainly refer to Israel. Isaiah 1:1 convinced me that what he "saw concerning Judah and Jerusalem" could not refer to the church, as I had always been taught. I now read Isaiah 61 also as not belonging to the church but as clearly describing the glory yet to be made manifest in Israel after her repentance and restoration to her own land. I had long contended against the premillenial advent but Luke 17:26-30; 2 Thessalonians 1:8 together with similar texts were opened to me with much power, clearly shewing that the present dispensation would end in judgment, *before* the period when the earth would be restored to blessing, and filled with the knowledge of the Lord. I asked myself how could "the day of the Lord come as a thief in the night," 2 Peter 3:10, if there was first to be a thousand years of blessing!

The evils connected with the various denominations into which the church of Christ is divided began also to occupy my thoughts. I had seen and heard much to convince me that many individuals who entered on the work of the ministry—dissenters as well as episcopalians—were unduly anxious to' increase their salaries, and too little concerned about feeding the flock, or leading sinners to Christ. I was gradually led to consider the example of the apostles, and the commendation bestowed on those who "went forth taking nothing of the gentiles," 3 John 7, and was convinced that those who labour for Christ in the gospel ought not to seek the help of the men of this world, but to rely on the care of Him who hath promised to supply His people's need. Philippians 4:19.

The practice of *seat rents* in places used for public worship, seemed to me unscriptural after James 2 was made plain to me. I had long before this seen the practical working of the system when the rent of the seat occupied by my family in the town where I resided, while I was labouring in the gospel elsewhere, was suddenly raised from one to two guineas a year, on the arrival of a new minister. I have no personal object in saying this, nor is it any pleasure to me to do so, but I feel bound to state plainly the circumstances by which I was gradually led to give up many things when they were shewn to me to be contrary to the word of God.

My mind was for some time undecided on the subject of Baptism. Being well versed in the arguments by which infant baptism is generally defended, it was some years after the first doubts concerning it arose in my mind, ere I became fully satisfied that it was altogether erroneous. My first doubts arose from hearing three sermons delivered by a talented minister in its defence, when I was surprised at the entire lack of Scripture proof in support of his argument, while he enlarged much on the inconvenience &c. of adult baptism. These were increasingly confirmed by his requesting me and others not to attend the one lecture to be given in reply by a baptist minister who had heard him. I was at length delivered from my painful uncertainty by perceiving from Romans 6:3-5 and many similar passages, how strikingly our union with Christ as being dead and risen with Him is set forth by immersion and also that Baptism is intended only for those who *believe* (Acts 8:37) which infants cannot do.

I have very briefly alluded to some of the subjects on which the Lord was now enlightening my mind, and preparing me for future service. The texts quoted are those which I well remember as occurring to me just at that time; and which appeared conclusive. Many others might be added equally important in reference to the same truths, but those named are sufficient for my present purpose.

While I was busily occupied with these subjects I began gradually to feel a degree of bondage, from being under the control and direction of those who appeared chiefly anxious to maintain

the respectability of their position in the church of God, and just
at this time a circumstance occurred which caused me much trial,
but eventually delivered me from my thraldom. A dear Christian
brother, by whose testimony the Lord has been greatly honoured,
came occasionally into the neighbourhood, and ministered on a
few occasions in the chapel at our village. I was sharply reproved
for this by the committee, and promised not to ask him again to
minister in any place under their control. I was afterwards rebuked
for attending his ministry in the open air; and subsequently told
that the committee could not allow their agent in any way to countenance this faithful servant of God. About this time I had some
counterbalance to my trial by the joy of witnessing four or five
conversions, but this grace and blessing of God appeared to be little
thought of by my employers, who were mainly occupied with the
subject alluded to. Yet strange as it may appear, they told me in the
committee they did not one of them know the brother alluded to,
nor had ever heard him minister, and that they believed him to be
"a very holy man of God!"

Whatever I had felt of my bondage before was nothing to this.
The question was *how could* I surrender my liberty by refusing to
acknowledge and countenance a dear servant of God at the mere
dictation of any man, or body of men? Carnal reason would have
replied "your maintenance, and that of your family depends on it."
But I was not permitted to listen to its dictates, and was soon made
cheerfully willing to leave the matter in the Lord's hands. I saw more
clearly than before that any order of things may be contended for
rather than the truth, and resolved from that time to give myself
to the work of the Lord as His servant to go only where HE might
direct me, and to seek from Him alone all that I might need for
my temporal support.

"If any man serve Me let him follow Me" John 12:26, is the
requirement of our heavenly master. The path of obedience is
marked out for us by His own example, and in seeking to walk
as He walked and to aim at His glory in all our imperfect service,

we shall find ample reward, whatever circumstances of trial such a confession of Him may be attended with. It will be enough to hear Him say at last "well done good and faithful servant."

Another subject which much pained me was the homage paid to individuals of wealth and influence. Some of the members of the association were men of the world, not even professing to be Christians, yet they had a voice in all the measures adopted. I have seen a gentleman in the chair at a Missionary Meeting held in a chapel, and heard him advocate the object about which they were assembled; yet he spent nearly the whole night at a hall near the same spot not long after.

I hope I do not say this in a censorious spirit. I esteem and honour all who seek to serve the Lord according to the measure of light and ability which He has given them; but I feel bound at the same time to state in simple honesty the events I have witnessed so far as they are needful to explain my own conduct in reference to the path I have taken.

A happy circumstance was connected with my quitting this place at the end of nearly three years. At the sale of my furniture a book was purchased by a young man, which led to his conversion. This same individual had caused the church bells to be rung the year previous, while I was preaching near his fathers house. He now became a decided witness for the truth, preaching the gospel in various places in the open air, and after a few years went as a missionary to India to declare the word of life to the perishing heathen. A missionary had thus been raised up in each of the two places in which I had hitherto laboured.

CHAPTER XII

THE RETURN

"What thou knowest not now thou shalt
know hereafter."—John 13:7

MY connection with the committee was to cease in four months from the time of their notice, during which I was kept free from anxiety, and waited on the Lord for guidance respecting the future. It was but three weeks previous to its expiration when I received a letter from a brother in the Lord, suggesting whether it might not be His will that I should again come to my native town, and labour in the surrounding villages until directed to some permanent place of service. I regarded this as the Lord's voice to me, and soon returned to occupy a cottage there. On receiving my last quarter's salary, and paying my rent and other debts, I had one shilling and three half pence remaining; a token as I then thought, that the Lord would supply my need, as He had hitherto done, and this was enough. But I determined from this time, never to contract debt for any purpose whatever, and I have rigidly adhered to it for the last twenty-five years, and have thus been spared a multitude of cares.

This was therefore a new era in my life, and with a family of nine persons, the prospect of being entirely cast on the providence of God, for their whole support, was not contemplated without some degree of anxiety, for I was led to choose this path not so much from a consciousness that I had faith to bear me out in it, but because I felt sure it was according to the Lord's mind, and that He would be honoured thereby, and would give me increasing faith as I went along, which I have since abundantly proved. It was attended at the commencement with sufficient trial to test the principles by which I professed to be guided, as will always be the case. The Lord will prove us, whatever the measure of grace He is pleased to bestow. On some occasions during the first year my faith and that of my sick wife, were severely tried, but the Lord's gracious deliverances, and very providential helps, were so timely, and so sweet, as to make the trial in its results a very happy one. Nor did either myself or my dear wife, during the short remainder of her life, which at this time was fast wasting by disease, (and this was by far my deepest trial) regret for one moment the resolution we had taken.

During the summer I preached in about thirty towns and villages, mostly in the open air. These places were from three to ten, and sometimes twenty miles from my residence, so that I frequently walked fifteen miles on the Lord's day and preached four times, and on some occasions I walked nearly thirty miles.

Towards the autumn my attention was especially drawn to two of these places, believing the Lord was about to direct my steps to one of them as my future place of abode. My only desire was to know His mind, being willing to go either to the village or the town, as He might direct me. This desire if *sincere,* is *never* disappointed.

I was at length assured that the village was the place where the gospel was most needed, and I continued to preach there once a fortnight, the time of my removal appearing uncertain, as there was no suitable house to be obtained. In my way to this place I sometimes passed through the village of Langridge Ford and once stayed there to preach, as I had time to spare. One of the inhabitants offered his cottage and I ministered with some liberty from Matthew 1:21. It was I believe, on my next visit when accompanied by S—— that we were invited by a poor woman, whose whole support was derived from the parish, to go to her cottage and partake of her *baked meat* (as she termed it) which we thankfully accepted. It consisted of a dish of baked potatoes with a small piece of bacon in the centre. There was also a small baked pudding on another dish. We much enjoyed the simple meal, which was made sweet by the kindness with which it was offered to us, as those who came in the name of the Lord. We remembered the promise that "whosoever shall give to drink unto one of these little ones a cup of cold water only in the name of a disciple, shall in no wise lose his reward"—Matthew 10:42, and we asked the Lord with some measure of faith that it might be realized by this poor woman. Our prayer was heard and answered. A few years after this, I had the joy of baptizing several of the inhabitants of this village (the fruit of subsequent ministry there) and among that number was this woman, her son in law, and two daughters, for like Rahab who received the spies with peace, the reward of her faith, extended not to herself only, but to her kindred and friends. (Joshua 6:25)

CHAPTER XIII

THE REVEL

"The works of the flesh, are drunkenness, revellings
and such like," &c.—Galatians 5:19-21

While on my way to a distant village at the close of the summer, I was overtaken by a woman on horseback. She was quite a stranger to me, and to my surprise, slackened her pace, and began to tell me of her unsuccessful errand to the town she had just quitted. She and her husband had recently been brought to know the truth through the ministry of some Wesleyans who came to preach m the village of Huncha, where many souls had been awakened, and she had been to request the Wesleyan minister to come and preach at their forthcoming Revel, the annual season, during which vice and iniquity with intemperance, abound in the villages of our land. She had however been disappointed, as he was expected elsewhere. As it was not to take place for ten days and I had no particular engagement, I offered to go and minister in his stead, which she gladly accepted. I requested two other brethren to accompany me, expecting much opposition. The place was ten miles from my home, and from the state of the weather and other causes, we were all much exercised, I may say *tempted* also, not to go. At length we were delivered, and arriving at the house of the sister I had previously seen took tea before the service.

It was a rough and stormy time, the enemy appearing determined to muster all his force to annoy us and hinder our purpose. Many who had lately been converted accompanied us to a spot very near the field in which the wrestling was to take place, and after singing a hymn and prayer by a brother who had not long before been himself a reveller there, I attempted to minister from "the wages of sin is death," &c. Romans 6:23. I scarcely remember ever to have had such power of voice as on this occasion, and often repeated the above words, which could be distinctly heard at the wrestling ring. This appears to have excited all the enmity of the poor revellers, who gradually gave up their sport and came down to annoy us. All the believers stood in a compact body on a small piece of rising ground, from which they sought by various means to drive us. While I was preaching the fiddler was sent for, and a dance was begun. About the same time some persons from behind the hedge began to fling earth and pieces of broken wood at us, and we were afterwards pelted with mud, until my clothes and the face of one of my companions was quite covered with it; we now found it impossible to continue to minister, but we still maintained our ground, conversing with those around us, some of whom seemed to lend a willing ear, which greatly encouraged us. Indeed the opposition arose mainly from some very rough men who had been deprived of their favorite amusement, while the spectators were generally favourable, and many of them wept to behold the savage treatment of their companions, who sometimes held their clenched fists close to my face, and others flung bowls at our legs, but the rising ground on which we stood preserved us from injury. At length our opponents suddenly left us, and went to the public house, when many gathered round us and lent a willing ear to some words of truth, after which we prayed with them and returned home.

I had never before witnessed such an open manifestation of the enmity of the carnal mind against the gospel of Christ, but doubted not that some blessing would result from our feeble testimony. I was encouraged in this feeling by the confession of the ringleader of the opposing party, who told me before he left I had made him commit "hundreds of sins" that evening. Perhaps he might afterwards have been made to feel that in all he had done he had been serving his master, "the god of this world." He was a daring character, and nothing appeared too vile for him. I heard afterwards that he was converted, but had no certain proof of this.

My hope of some happy result was not disappointed. Two of the brethren from that place called on me some time after, one of whom informed me with much joy that his son was converted through the ministry of that evening. Truly our God *does* constrain "the wrath of man to praise Him," and no one purpose of His mercy shall be hindered by all the power of Satan or the enmity of wicked men.

I was called in the following year to witness another painful scene. After preaching for several successive days in different towns, I was returning home, and coming near Crediton was led to ask the Lord's mind about tarrying the night and preaching the gospel. On coming into the town I found it was the fair day, and being asked to remain and minister I considered the invitation as the Lord's reply. This place was noted for the cruel sport of bull-baiting, which had not then been entirely banished from our land. Many dear saints accompanied me to a spot between the green, where the bull-baiting was held, and what was termed the pleasure fair. We commenced by singing

"Jesus! and shall it ever be
A mortal man ashamed of thee?"

but had not proceeded far with the service, when the poor gored animal was led through the town, and purposely brought out from the centre of the road to disturb us. Tamed by his sufferings, he appeared quite harmless, and came very near the chair on which I stood, when a man who was returning from his work struck it with a firkin which he had in his hand in order to turn it away from us. This led to a fight between him and the owner of the animal, and blood soon flowed. As it was impossible to proceed, I went into a house until the tumult subsided when about two hundred persons soon gathered together. After singing two verses commencing with

> "Our Jesus shall be still our theme
> While in this world we stay,"

I was enabled to speak with liberty from 1 Peter 1:18-19, no one making the least disturbance. An aged man from the country was heard to say to himself "Ah! I *know* it is *all true.*"

CHAPTER XIV

THE MISSIONARY TOUR

"And it came to pass that He went throughout
every city and village preaching the glad tidings
of the kingdom of God."—Luke 8:1

IN the summer of this year I accompanied a beloved brother on a short missionary excursion into some destitute villages of our neighbourhood. We were without purse or scrip and had no settled plan for our journey, our object being to preach the gospel, distribute, tracts, and ascertain the moral condition of the people. About noon on the first day we preached at Chittlehamholt, a village three miles from the parish church; the inhabitants were noted for lawlessness, having driven away all who had before attempted to minister there; yet about thirty persons heard with attention and a house was offered for preaching. More will be said of this place ere long. In the evening we preached in Chittlehampton, the church-town—as it was called—of the same parish, which being under high aristocratic influence no house had been used for preaching there within the memory of any inhabitant, and the rain prevented our ministering out of doors. In this emergency the Lord provided for our need. A cottage which had been quitted *that same day* was offered us, and crowded with attentive hearers. On the second day a large company belonging to a club assembled to hear the word at High

Bickington, after which we walked until day light, being unable to discern any shed to lie down in, and the rain falling during the greater part of the night. Having lost our way, we found ourselves in the morning near Winckleigh, a small town where the word was preached at nine o'clock. Here dwelt one family of disciples, who received us gladly. On the morning of the fourth day we again lost our way and wandered to the small village of Kingscot, where our hearts were much cheered by finding many dear Christians; with whom we had a short season of happy communion. The news of our arrival spread so rapidly that thirty persons were soon gathered in one of the cottages to hear the word of life. We then went to the village of St. Giles, two miles distant, where we purposed to spend the evening and my dear companion preached with great power to about one hundred persons. One of them, who came from the village where we tarried in the morning, was converted; so that our mistake in losing our way, through which our meeting was known at that place, was used by the Lord for bringing a soul to Himself. How wonderful are the ways of our God, who causes all events to fulfil His own blessed purposes! This village was very near the mansion of the most influential nobleman in the county, whose decided dislike to all public worship except that of the establishment was well known, and in the whole surrounding district which formed a part of his vast possessions, his word was considered almost as law; he is now dead, and his title extinct. Being greatly interested in the appearance of the people, I gave notice of a second service on that day fortnight, though the place was ten miles from my home. Two dear brethren accompanied me on this second visit, when many again assembled, while some individuals endeavoured in various ways to annoy us. The regular ringers, it is true, refused to ring the church bells to drown our voices, but some young learners made noise enough to answer that purpose. We were delivered from, this in a very singular manner. The clergyman, riding to the church gate where we were assembled, and giving his horse in charge to one of the hearers, hastened to the church tower, where he stopped the hells in much anger, supposing they were rung to *compliment,* instead of to disturb us! On going to the inn for a pony on which one of my companions had ridden, we were grossly abused by the schoolmaster of the place. The poor man's arm was in a sling, and we were afterwards told that he had intended to get up a dance on the green when we came to preach, and had offered sixpence to each person who would join while he played the fiddle. But the Lord interfered; he was thrown from his horse in the meantime, and the arm which was to have been used in the service of Satan was disabled. How oft is that solemn word fulfilled "The wrath of man shall praise Thee, and the remainder thereof shalt thou restrain." Psalm 76:10.

I felt encouraged to give notice of a third service, and on coming to the village on that occasion I found that the publican could neither receive my horse at the inn or sell me any refreshment, having offended the clergyman by doing so before, and by allowing his family to attend the preaching. This however did not discourage me, as I generally went on foot, and when I again rode the Lord provided my horse a shelter. Having a shoe loose I took him to the blacksmith, who kindly offered me to leave him there at any time and refused to be paid for his labour. The Lord had touched this man's heart, and he refused to work while I was preaching. I believe he was one of the first converts there. On this third visit the schoolmaster rode into our midst, and tried by every means to make his horse plunge and kick to disturb us. The people generally were however favorable to the gospel, but no one as yet ventured to ask me into his house lest he should incur the displeasure of the great, so that I have walked the whole distance out and home without any intermediate rest. But in the end I was richly repaid for my toil and labour.

When the approach of autumn prevented preaching in the open air, I was still anxious, and I may say *impelled,* to continue my labours at this village. There was no way to accomplish this so as not to interfere with my other duties except by a short service early on the Lord's day, which I continued until the middle of November, at half-past nine in the morning, at the gate of the church yard. The interesting results will soon be related in the "converted publican."

As a specimen of the ignorance which we met with on our tour— One poor man, when asked if he knew Jesus, replied "he had often *heard* of the man, but had never *seen* Him yet; but he hoped he should some day." At another place, a deaf woman mistook us for quack doctors, and thought our tracts were papers to recommend our medicines, perhaps from never having seen any before. We were much touched with the sufferings of another very afflicted woman, and asked if she wished us to pray with her, when she burst into tears, and said with much feeling *"she had nothing to pay us!"*

CHAPTER XV

A NEW SCENE OF SERVICE

"I will be with thee in all places whither
thou, goest,"—Genesis 28:13

AFTER a residence of nine months at Barnstaple I saw clearly it was the Lord's will I should go to High Bickington. There was however one great difficulty, as no convenient house could be obtained. The health of my beloved wife was fast declining, but her heart was so much set on going there, and as we fondly hoped she might derive benefit from the change, we were content to reside for a time in very incommodious lodgings.

I was prepared to enter on this new field of service as a pilgrim, and was soon made to feel myself one to an extent I had not anticipated. Leaving many dear friends behind, I was cast among strangers, of whom the majority were scorners, immoral and profane; with only three or four individuals who knew the Lord.

My last evening previous to removal was spent with some dear Christians, who met with me for prayer at the cottage of S——, at Loveacot. At parting, one of them said to me "I have set before thee an open door and no man can shut it," Revelation 3:8, and it was a word of strength and encouragement to me, as from the Lord Himself. It was much in my thought while journeying the next day to my future home, where my dear wife had preceded me; and it was the text of my first sermon there. It was also prophetically true, as I afterwards proved to my great joy.

The Lord, who knew how much I needed encouragement and comfort, was graciously pleased soon to cheer my spirit. I had only arrived a few hours when I was informed of the great change in the conduct of a poor man who had been accustomed to attend the ministry. I called on him immediately, and found him deeply convinced of sin and anxious to find peace with God, which was ere long granted. He said he had very seldom gone to any place of worship till he was led from curiosity to go to the cottage; his usual practice on Lord's day being to retain his working dress, and seldom even to shave till the evening; much of the afternoon was spent in his *pig's house,* where he would sit on a stool and worship his unclean idol, frequently combing it! We need not contemplate a more disgusting picture of moral depravity in this so-called Christian land, yet are there many equally debased.

This man was the first-fruit of my labour in the gospel at High Bickington. My beloved wife, during her brief sojourn there, was also used by the Lord in the awakening of a dear girl, who came with some others to a meeting for reading the scriptures which she held soon after her arrival.

It was also at this time, when surrounded with outward trials, that the Lord began to teach me somewhat more fully the evils of my own heart. It will appear strange to some that after having known the Lord nearly twenty years, and having been used by Him as an instrument of blessing to many souls, I should have known but little comparatively of *myself.* I could not yet understand how the most honoured of the apostles could call himself "tho chief of sinners," 1 Timothy 1:15 and "less than the least of all saints." Ephesians 3:8. But the Lord was now opening to me the secret "chambers of imagery," Ezekiel 8:12, and causing me to say with Job in a manner I never did before, "I have heard of thee by the hearing of the ear, but now mine eye seeth thee, wherefore I abhor myself and repent in dust and ashes." Job 42:5. The Lord knew how greatly I needed this increase of *self*-knowledge, and while the discipline was deeply painful I could heartily praise Him for it all, being enabled thereby to minister with greater liberty and clearness the truth of His own word.

The great trial so long anticipated soon came upon me. Within two months after our removal to High Bickington, the Lord was pleased to take my dear wife to Himself. She had previously been carried to her father's house, for the benefit of the kind attentions of her dear sisters, who watched over her with great tenderness. I was now a pilgrim indeed! But great as was my sorrow, it was not permitted to overwhelm me. My six children were scattered, and thus all my domestic joys taken away, just when I was more than ever in a land of strangers. My beloved and very aged mother was also taken hence a few weeks before. I should not notice these family trials, did it not seem necessary, in order to show the peculiar circumstances in which I was placed after entering on a new path of service, with no source of help or dependence save the *living God*.

Through the kindness of friends my dear children were in various ways cared for, by being sent to school, &c. so that my deep and painful bereavement left me at liberty to give my whole time to the Lord's work, in pursuing which I found my chief comfort and joy. I had much to be thankful for in this respect. I had taken a large cellar and fitted it up for preaching the gospel. It accommodated about a hundred persons, though many more crowded within its walls every Lord's day evening, some of whom from the very commencement evinced their attachment to the gospel.

When I retrace this sorrowful period of my life, I seem to wonder that I was sustained through it; but our poor hearts are very prone to mistrust the power and grace of Him who has promised strength equal to our day. Through His abounding mercy I was never permitted for one moment to murmur or repine, or to doubt that all was sent in love by Him who is able to do for us "exceeding abundantly, above all we ask or think, according to the power that worketh in us." Ephesians 3:20.

My coming to High Bickington appeared to excite in no common degree the enmity of the servants of sin. Many hearts which had hitherto been under the dominion of "the strong man armed" were about to own the sway of Him who is stronger than he, and great efforts were made to retain them. Vain amusements abounded more during the summer of this year than at any previous period. The village band was often engaged; wrestling and cockfighting, together with their favorite amusement of bell-ringing were frequent, and at the annual fair some low comedians were hired from a distance to take part in a masquerade, which was kept up several successive nights. One of them personifying Satan, (who was himself much nearer than they were aware of), and suddenly appearing in the company, one of the party was greatly frightened, and became seriously ill. There seemed to be no bounds to their sin and folly at this season, during which the Lord was working in *the hearts of many*, the seed of the word having taken root.

I had been there but a few weeks, when it occurred to me that a service on the morning of the Lord's day might be useful. I was strongly dissuaded from this, and told that as the cellar in which we met was close to the gate of the church yard, no one would attend. But feeling assured that it would eventually work for good, it was commenced. At first it was attended by only four or five persons besides the children of the Sunday school, who were instructed by two young persons, who were the only believers I then knew in the village except the poor man whose conversion has been related. But the number gradually increased, until at the end of the summer we had from twenty to thirty adult hearers, some of whom were hopeful enquirers. On the whole I had much cause for thankfulness in the prospect before me.

While thus rejoicing in the progress of the Lord's work and the sure hope of future blessing on my labours, I was subjected to much scorn and contempt from the openly wicked; one instance of which may be noticed. When once on my way to the evening prayer meeting, I was accosted by the overseer of the parish, who requested me to go before a magistrate, and on my enquiring for what purpose, he said I was but recently come into the parish, where I might perhaps gain a settlement, and eventually be a burthen to them by requiring support. He therefore wished me to go and state my circumstances. I expressed my readiness and asked for his summons; he said he had no summons but thought I ought to go without requiring one!

This poor man was made drunk for the purpose, and chose a time when the village band were near enough to be within hearing. He was a farmer, and his habits of intemperance had undermined his health. He died not long afterwards of consumption. I once called at his house and endeavoured to set the truth of the gospel before him, but my offer to pray was rejected, saying that he should give offence to his friends by permitting it. How truly was it thus made manifest that "the god of this world hath blinded the minds of them which believe not, lest the light of the knowledge of the Gospel of Christ should shine unto them." 2 Corinthians 4:4

CHAPTER XVI

THE LITTLE FARM

"I can do all things through Christ which strengthened me."—Philippians 4:13

AMONG the earliest and most attentive hearers of the gospel were C—— C—— and his wife, who lived at a small farm on the border of the village. I have called it the "little farm," being only about thirty acres in extent, and its name also was "Little Bickington." The family consisted of only four persons; the parents, their young child, and a servant. The farm house was merely a cottage, containing a kitchen, three bed rooms, and a small parlour, seven feet by ten, the fire-place being in one corner. The last act of my beloved wife previous to her leaving was to seek a lodging for me there, which was readily granted. The accommodation was of a very humble character, but notwithstanding the lack of many comforts to which I had previously been accustomed, I spent in this lowly dwelling some of the happiest days of my life; for I had never seen such manifest blessing on the Lord's work in so short a period. The dear farmer and his wife were most kind; they sought by every means in their power to promote my comfort, and were always willing to listen to the truth. I soon had cause to bless God that I was led to tarry under their roof. Six weeks after my arrival I was one day surprised and gladdened by seeing my kind host enter my room after dinner, and by his expressing a desire that I would pray with him. The Lord had deeply convinced both himself and his wife of sin, and from this time I had the fullest confidence that He would grant them the joy of His salvation, which was very soon realized. A poor woman also, who occasionally came there to work was converted. My joy at this time was such as caused me often to forget my sorrows; for I looked on this as the earnest of an approaching harvest. Soon after their conversion it occurred to me while in bed, that my dear friends would probably have some trial of their faith, as a counterbalance to their present joy, and to prove the reality of the Lord's work in their souls. They had but one horse, which was an excellent animal and quite young, and the thought came suddenly into my mind "what if they should lose their horse?" To my great surprise, Christopher remarked the *next day* that "the horse did not eat his hay last night," but as he went through his day's work as usual no further notice was taken of it; on the following day, however, he was decidedly ill, but no danger was apprehended. On the third day the farrier was sent for, but the disease baffled all his skill, and the poor animal died on the fourth day after the thought concerning him had first crossed my mind. It was a severe stroke to my dear friends, who could not replace the loss without difficulty, but they abundantly proved that "the joy of the Lord was their strength," so that the sorrow which had been otherwise so great, was counterbalanced by the knowledge that it was appointed by infinite wisdom and love. I was anxious to give them some small token of my sympathy by helping towards the purchase of another horse. This was not then in my power, but the Lord in a very providential manner sent me the needful help. When Christopher was afterwards on his way to the farrier a letter was given to him for me containing five pounds, a much larger sum than I had ever before received at one time from the same person. I was thus enabled to show my dear friends the kindness I had desired. When I revisited this place three years ago

I found to my joy that their dear son also had been converted and was walking happily in the good ways of the Lord.

After a residence of two years at "the little farm" I felt desirous to have at least one of my dear children with me, and being unable to procure a suitable house I took a small cottage containing only a kitchen and two bed rooms, and here my dear eldest daughter resided with me until a more convenient house was erected about a year after. I was here made to prove that "a man's life consisteth not in the abundance of the things which he possesseth." The great Secret of happiness consists in having a *subdued will*, a *single eye*, and a *conscience void of offence*, the root of all being faith in Christ Jesus. Had I waited for a *convenient habitation* I should never have gone to High Bickington, but should have lost the blessing I enjoyed there of witnessing the conversion of *many* souls. The joy connected with *this* is lasting and eternal.

While on a visit during the summer of this year to a neighbourhood for which I had strong attachment, and where the prospect of usefulness was promising, I was asked by two kind friends whether it might not be the Lord's will for me to fix my residence there. A house was already provided, and my future support would cease to be a matter of uncertainty; but the Lord did not suffer me to yield to the temptation. My immediate reply was that the cloud had pitched at High Bickington, and had not since moved. See Numbers 9:17-28. It was not long after this when the Lord's presence was plainly discerned, and my heart rejoiced by witnessing the conversion of many souls to Himself. I have for a long time been fully assured that whatever we are made willing to give up of personal comfort or convenience for the Lord's sake, while seeking to serve Him in the gospel, will always *sooner* or *later* be rewarded by His giving us the desire of our hearts.

> "I thank thee Lord thy cross hath made
> This world a wilderness to me;
> While all the daily path I tread,
> Is still the road that leads to thee.

My risen Saviour and my God,
    Thy glory is alone my aim;
The path m sorrow thou hast trod,
    And I would meekly tread the same.

Whate'er impedes me on the way,
    Or would to earth my soul incline,
Take, I beseech thee, take away,
    And make me, Saviour, wholly thine."
                        —A. H.

CHAPTER XVII

THE CONVERTED PUBLICAN

"I am the Lord the God of all flesh; is there
anything too hard for me?"—Jeremiah 32:27

IN the spring of this year I again visited St. Giles, according to
my promise the previous autumn; and on no previous occasion
had my heart been more gladdened, than by the reception I
now met with. The inhabitants were no longer shy of admitting me
into their houses, and a great change had evidently taken place in
the minds of many. Since my last visit several of them had gone on
the Lord's day to a neighboring town to hear the gospel, and not
a few had been awakened to serious enquiry. Being informed that
the publican would now be glad to see me, I went to his house, and
cannot describe the joy I experienced at finding both him and his
wife anxiously desiring to get peace, and their two sons converted.
Instead of refusing to *sell* me any refreshment, whatever I needed
was now *freely offered without charge;* and I seldom called without being pressed to partake of their hospitality. The conversion of
this family was an event of importance. Mr. B—— was a highly
respectable person, following the several trades of publican, miller,
wheelwright, and shopkeeper, and was thus in a great measure independent of those who might wish to injure him on account of his
faithful testimony to the truth, which he immediately began to

exhibit. Resolving to conduct his business in the fear of the Lord he allowed no excess in his house, nor would he sell any beer on the Lord's day, except to travellers; and at their next revel, the lovers of sinful pleasure were much disappointed by his refusal to sell any beer during the whole day; and as there was no other inn in the village, they were obliged to send two miles to procure it. All the influence of the rich could not hinder the power of the truth in the minds of many. An early prayer meeting was held at six on Lord's day mornings to avoid publicity; and a Sunday school was soon established. Being invited by a poor man who had a spare room in his cottage I once slept there after the service, and on retiring late to rest I heard several persons in the street talking about the sermon they had heard, and recognised the voice of the black smith before alluded to, inviting some one to begin to pray and read the Bible.

I continued to go there during this summer, after which the work was taken up by the Wesleyans, my own service nearer home being sufficient to occupy all my time. The publican's sincere desire to promote the gospel, uninfluenced by the fear of man, was very apparent. The whole village and its neighbourhood were the property of Lord R——, but the premises occupied by Mr. B—— were full leased for four lives, and in a short time he resolved to build a small chapel in the garden before his house. That an *innkeeper* should do this, at his *own expense,* is perhaps almost an unprecedented occurrence, especially under the circumstances in which he was placed, and the opposition he expected to meet with. But he had been delivered from that fear of man which bringeth temptation and a snare, and was made willing to endure reproach and persecution for the sake of the gospel.

From the time of my leaving High Bickington I heard no tidings of the progress of the Lord's work in this place, until about three years ago, when on being requested by a company of believers to give some account of my past labours in the gospel, the love and zeal of this believing publican were mentioned. On the following day I was informed by one of the brethren who had been present, that he was himself in the employ of Lord R—— twenty years ago, and had sometimes heard me preach at the church gate in St. Giles, but he did not recognise my person on the preceding evening, till I alluded to the circumstances which he so well remembered. The wife of this brother was related by marriage to the publican's family, and I was thankful to learn from him that the Lord's work at St. Giles had continued to prosper notwithstanding much opposition, and that the little chapel had been enlarged to accommodate an increased number of hearers. The publican had continued to support the gospel, but had given up the business of an innkeeper.

CHAPTER XVIII

THE CONTRAST

"For we are unto God a sweet savour of Christ
in them that are saved, and in them that
perish," &c.—2 Corinthians 2:15-16

EARLY in the summer of this year it was laid on my heart
to go to Roborough, one of the villages visited by myself
and my dear companion last year. My feelings on entering
it on *that* occasion were very peculiar, such as I had never before
experienced. It seemed as though the powers of darkness were near
me, and busily active in opposing our entrance; and all we saw of
the people was discouraging, beyond anything we had witnessed
elsewhere. On the present occasion I had sent notice of my intention to preach, and given tracts to the messenger to distribute
previous to my arrival, but on coming there I was told that various threatenings had been heard, and that I might be interrupted
by stones and rotten eggs if I attempted to preach. But the Lord
restrained this open manifestation of their rage, by causing me to
meet a farmer of whom I had some knowledge, and who had much
influence in the village. He was a vile character, but came from
curiosity to hear me. The Lord's hand was discernable here, as he
lived at some distance, and met me just at the needed time. My
subsequent visits for the next two years were *most* discouraging, nor

have I ever seen a place which manifested more entire, hardness of heart and enmity to the gospel.

A second village, which exhibits a striking contrast to the above, was the first in which we preached on the tour above alluded to. The inhabitants of both were equally ignorant and profane, and equally noted for their hatred to the gospel. A week after my visit to Roborough it was strongly impressed on my mind while dressing, that I must go and preach that evening at Chittlehamholt, and a friend who knew the road kindly consented to go with me. The distance of five miles was intersected by a river, half way on the road, which had to be crossed by a ferry. The people here seemed prepared to receive the gospel, and the preaching was attended by many hearers, some of whom showed much desire for its continuance, and invited me to their houses, one of which was offered for ministry. It appeared even at this first visit as though the time to favour this hitherto dark neighbourhood was now come, especially as they had up to the period of our previous visit resisted every attempt to introduce the gospel there. I continued to go there regularly during the summer and following winter, when the cottage was generally crowded to excess, and the Lord was evidently causing the seed sown to take root in many hearts. In the following spring a dear brother in the Lord went to reside there. His first sermon having been used by the Lord in converting one of the hearers, from this time conversions, became numerous, and many were gathered into communion. As I had abundant employment elsewhere, my future service at this place was only occasional, but the history of the Lord's work there is sufficiently interesting to be noticed, though it will necessarily extend beyond the time of which I am writing.

The labours of the brother alluded to were abundantly prospered, so that about fifty children of God used to meet at this table to

> SCRIPTURE TESTIMONY
>
> *The sheep know and hear His voice*
>
> JOHN 10:3-4 · JOHN 10:16

commemorate the dying love of Jesus. It soon became necessary to erect a chapel, a work which was much furthered by a gentleman who had property in the village, and who kindly gave the land and also the stones for the building; he was led to do this from perceiving the moral influence produced by the preaching of the gospel. Very different was the conduct of others, who became alarmed at the attempt to enlighten the poor by any instrumentality save that of the Establishment. Up to this time no effort of any kind had been made to promote their spiritual welfare, but I had not been long there when the erection of a school room was commenced, in which the clergyman ministered every Lord's day evening. The nobleman who lived near St. Giles had also large possessions in this neighbourhood, and his sisters lived only a mile or two from the village, but the poor villagers still continued their attendance, attracted by the simple tidings of the gospel of the grace of God. When it was found that the school room was not well attended a church was built, and the occasional visits of a curate were exchanged for a resident clergyman. Yet the word of the Lord continued to prosper, and has done so I believe to the present time.

The remarkable contrast between the two places noticed in this chapter may suggest an important enquiry. Whence is it that while to all outward appearance there was such a great similarity, the gospel was so gladly received at one place, and so entirely rejected at the other? The word of God can alone help us in this enquiry. Paul and Silas were forbidden to preach the word in Asia, and were not allowed to go into Bithynia, but when invited through a vision to go to Macedonia, they went, assuredly gathering that the Lord had called them to preach the gospel *there,* (Acts 16:6-10) and there they found that harvest of blessing which they so desired to reap. Is it not thus the Lord causes it to "rain on one city not on another?" Amos 4:7, and are not these among the deep things of God respecting which the Lord says "Even so, Father, for so it seemeth good in thy sight?" Matthew 11:26. The sudden impulse through which I was led to the village where the gospel was so gladly welcomed and made a blessing to many souls, I have always judged to have come from the Lord.

An interesting fact has lately come to my knowledge respecting that neighbourhood. The ancestors of the family whose influence was now so painfully used to hinder the gospel, were once its zealous supporters, and the mansion in which part of the family resided near Chittlehamholt, was an asylum for the persecuted nonconformists of former days. The following interesting passage is from a volume entitled "Spiritual Heroes."

"The nonconformists in country villages sometimes avoided detection by assembling in some manorial hall belonging to one of the richer brethren; and there, at the midnight hour, the ejected pastor gathered round him some of the scattered flock, and refreshed their hearts by the sound of his familiar voice, but infinitely more by the truths he uttered. There, in the great hall of Hudscot, belonging to the family of the Holies, near South Molton, John Flavel addressed a crowded auditory, supported by the hospitality, and surrounded by the influence of the owner of the mansion. He resided there for some time, and amidst the plantations, gardens, and rural scenes, which environed the spot, gathered the materials for his ' Husbandry Spiritualized,' so that it is highly probable that he furnished in his midnight exercises many of those ingenious illustrations, so suited to the tastes and habits of his rustic flock, which are found in the popular work just mentioned. The recesses of the dark wood afforded a still more secure, and in some seasons a more grateful, sanctuary, and beneath the deep shade of lofty pines or overhanging elms, or round the gnarled trunks of oaks that had stood for ages, forming temples of Gods own buildings, the persecuted brotherhood assembled to hear the word of God; and there too at times, without fear and as freely as the birds in the branches, would they lift their voices to heaven, and chant the high praises of their Creator."

CHAPTER XIX

HARVEST TIME

"Say not ye, There are yet four months, and then
cometh harvest? behold. I say unto you, Lift
up your eyes, and look on the fields; for they
are white already to harvest."—John 4:35

THOSE who have witnessed the cheerful operations of the
harvest field in some parts of our land, where busy groups,
with light hearts, are engaged in gathering the fruits of the
earth, will be at no loss to understand why the scriptures allude to
"the joy of harvest" Isaiah 9:18; the Lord having used the same figure
in reference to the higher joy of beholding souls gathered to Himself.
If the pleasure of seeing many souls converted to God within a short
period, may be as beholding "the fields white unto harvest," it has
been my privilege on different occasions to realise it, and this was
especially the case at High Bickington towards the close of 1833.

This happy season commenced about nine months after I dame
to reside there, and continued through the dreary period of the
succeeding winter, during which a week seldom passed without
hearing of one or more cases of deep conviction through the power
of the Spirit accompanying the word of truth.

There was a small hamlet consisting of only three houses, one
mile and a half from the village, where this power was especially

manifested. The occupier of one of these was the tenant of a small farm, and a great favourite with the pleasure loving inhabitants of our village, to whose amusement he largely contributed. He was the chief ringer of the church bells, the leading singer in the church gallery, and a performer in the village band. Being cheerful and of ready wit the alehouse was soon filled when it was known that he was there, The calling of such an one to follow a rejected and despised Saviour, and to be a faithful witness for His truth, caused great alarm in the ranks of the enemy, for it was made manifest that there was a power at work among them such as they could not resist.

It was scarcely two months after his conversion when, on a Lord's day evening, he told me with much joy that his wife had received blessing through the ministry in the morning from Mark 4:26-29, and it proved to be a work of real conversion.

A circumstance which occurred soon after, showed how truly he desired to honour the Lord by his testimony. A gentleman who had come to the village to hunt and shoot on his estates, which lay near it, wished him to be a witness against another gentleman whom our brother had seen trespassing on his grounds. But this new convert felt constrained to refuse, and in a long conversation with the gentleman (who had power to do him much injury), showed him from the Lord's Prayer, that if *we* expect forgiveness we ought to forgive *others*. Although the gentleman alluded to was displeased and disappointed in not being able to revenge himself on the trespasser, who was his personal enemy, the Lord did not permit him in any way to use his influence to the injury of His dear servant.

In the second house of the hamlet the aged father and mother of this brother resided with their unmarried daughter. The two latter were also among the number of the early converts.

Of the third family, the greater number were brought to the knowledge of Christ during this winter. That portion of it which resided at home, was the father, mother, an only son, and three daughters, two other daughters who were married lived in and near the village. Of this number, four of the daughters and their aged mother were early converted, and the other daughter and her only son some time after. The son also became so deeply convinced of sin that he could no longer continue with the ringers, and being the second best of their number, the loss of their two best men prevented them from ringing for a prize after this time, which they had hitherto done with much renown. He was first awakened through hearing a sermon on the power of conscience, as exhibited in Felix when Paul reasoned before him on "righteousness, temperance, and judgment to come." Acts 24:25. On leaving the room, I was laid hold of by some one who said he wanted to speak with me. It was quite dark, and this young man (who was noted for fighting and quarrelling, and used to boast that he had never been beaten) accompanied by some vain companions, began to tell me what he had felt during the sermon. The only expression used by him that I distinctly remember, was sufficiently indicative of his natural character, which was bold daring, and honest. "I *tell you what,* sir, I have got a conscience, and I can't obey it." Never were words more truly spoken, as his whole subsequent course has painfully proved, while there is yet confident hope that he has never altogether lost the impressions of that evening.

Of the three unmarried daughters, the two youngest were twins, and being the children of her old age they were the especial favourites of their dear mother. The grace of Rachel[5] and Mary was observed and acknowledged by all. But I shall have occasion again to write about the dear mother and her darling daughters very soon.

The eldest daughter of this favoured family lived in the village, and with her husband and their two children, were also converted.

---

5   At the time I wrote this, Rachel had just been taken to be with Christ, only one week previous to the expected arrival of her beloved sister, (from whom she had been living at some distance since the marriage of the latter) to come and reside once more near her former home. Her sorrowing husband in a letter received from him a few day ago, writes that "after being four days in bed, she was taken to be absent from the body, and present with the Lord." During this time, her soul was so happy, so quiet, resting on the finished work of Christ, that she was enabled to triumph over death. "She has now no more the mingled cup, but is for ever with the Lord."

Like Martha she was "careful, and troubled about many things." So thrifty and industrious was she naturally, as to be often at her gloving work at three in the mornings; and if she was expecting to wash on Monday, the water was fetched from the well on the Lord's day evening. Of course it was out of the question to attend a week evening service, as time in her estimation was so precious. It is however written "Thy people shall be willing in the day of Thy power," Psalm 110:3 and this is as true respecting every sinner called by divine grace to follow Christ now as it will be of the whole Jewish nation when that Psalm has its fulfilment. It was one day impressed on her mind, that she must go to the room that evening, and from that evening she dated her conversion to God. She became indeed "a new creature," called to follow Christ so fully that the change was manifest to all. We do not always behold, even in advanced Christians, the graces that are directly

SCRIPTURE TESTIMONY
Salvation transforms
2 CORINTHIANS 5:16-17 · GALATIANS 6:15

opposed to their former character, but in the present instance, the over carefulness about worldly things vanished away, and it was succeeded by the most generous hospitality. For many years she delighted to deny herself during the week, that she might keep an open table at tea time every Lord's day, for all saints who might have come from a distance, and wished to be present at the evening service. I have oftentimes met the happy company on these occasions. Precious also were the prayer meetings at Shutely, the hamlet where three fourths of the adult population had recently been converted to God, and were just in the enjoyment of their first love. But changes have since taken place, and the three families have all removed elsewhere.

I have dwelt chiefly on these conversions, as being the most interesting, but they are only a part of the many. Three dear youths, of the several trades of mason, carpenter, and shoemaker, were converted nearly at the same time, in this winter; and one of them the bereaved husband of Rachel, has been a greatly honoured instrument in carrying on the work of the Lord, during the eighteen years I have left them.

Nothing has yet been said of the poor father of that dear family, whose hardness of heart and bitter enmity to the truth, formed such a painful contrast to the grace he constantly witnessed in his dear wife and children. The innumerable trials they endured for their attachment to the gospel, can only be known to themselves, and to Him whom they confessed and served with unflinching firmness, and who was dearer to them than all besides. The father was generally absent from home on business nearly half the week, and then only they had peace; if the scriptures were attempted to be read at night, the candle was blown out; one of his daughters was thrown down stairs, when found by him on her knees; he rarely returned from the village sober, and on market days we generally heard him on his return, roaring and blaspheming, long before he passed our door. I was the especial object of his hatred. He always spoke of me as the devil, and called our chapel the gaol. When he once heard that I was passing through the hamlet late on a summers evening, he left his bed nearly naked, and came to his door to curse me as I passed along. On two occasions his poor wife was dragged from our place of meeting, and he once came into the house opposite his own while we were holding a prayer meeting and forced away his two daughters, one of whom soon returned with her head bleeding from being knocked against a wall. As I did not fear his violence, I never went out of my way to avoid him, though sometimes entreated to do so, and only

> **SCRIPTURE TESTIMONY**
>
> *Beaten for preaching the Gospel*
>
> ACTS 5:40 · ACTS 14:19-20

once did he attempt to do me injury. He was at that time much intoxicated, when he got hold of me, threw me down, and was beginning to kick and beat me. He was, however, hindered by his son, who collared his poor father till I was out of his reach. In consequence of this he sustained much injury from the kicks and blows of his enraged parent, so that for two or three days he was unable to return home, and remained at my house which was not far distant. On becoming sober the poor man told his son he had saved him from the gallows, as he believed he should have killed me had he not been prevented by his interference.

I omitted to state in its proper place, that the daughter who was so worldly minded previous to her conversion, was after a few years unable to pursue her needle-work through the growing imperfection of her sight. At this time a Christian lady offered her a home in her house, which she declined, as she did also the kind offer of the loan of a sum of money to enable her to support herself by a small business. She preferred waiting on the Lord about her future path, and He directed her in the way which she should go. By the death of her husband she became possessed of a few pounds which were due from the club of which he was a member, and with this she opened a small shop, desiring to conduct it in the fear of the Lord. And it may truly he said that the Lord was with her. She fully proved the truth of the promise "them that honour me I will honour," 1 Samuel 2:80 being so prospered that from a small beginning she had at length the largest shop in the village. She determined from the first to act as far as possible on the principle of owing no man anything, and with the exception of only one article, which is paid for quarterly when the traveller comes to her house, every particle of the stock is her own. She seeks to honour the Lord with her substance according to her ability, and she has realised the truth that "there is that scattereth and yet increaseth," while very many alas! are equally proving to their sorrow that "there is that witholdeth more than is meet, and it tendeth to poverty." Proverbs 11:24

> I am not skilled to heal disease,
> Or set the fractured limb;
> I cannot strait the crippled knee,
> Or clear the eye ball dim;
> But I may ply that art divine,
> The art to pour the oil and wine.

The man of learning and of parts,
　　Soars far above my path;
I cannot cope with stately hearts,
　　Who scorn my ember hearth;
Be mine while in this dreary wild,
The lot to bless the poor man's child.

CHAPTER XX

THE BAPTISM

"Know ye not that many of us as were baptized unto Jesus
Christ, were baptized into His death?"—Romans 6:3

I HAVE seldom anticipated a day of trial with more anxiety than
that on which I expected to baptise a few of the saints who had
been lately converted. They were to be baptised in a river two
miles from the village, on Good Friday, being the anniversary of
the day when I had myself confessed the Lord in the same river, in
the presence of about a thousand persons. Many things concurred
to depress my mind on this occasion. It was the first time I had
been asked to baptise any of the Lord's people, and I knew that
this solemn ordinance was exceedingly despised by the ignorant
and depraved population around me who had never yet witnessed
this new thing; added to this I had a severe cold and the weather
was bleak and wintry. Two of the candidates had colds also. I doubt
not that much of my own feeling arose from temptation, which a
stronger faith would have resisted and overcome; there was however
a bright contrast between the fears of the morning and the happy
conclusion of that memorable day.

Rachel and Mary were among those who wished to make this
open profession of their faith in Jesus to the great sorrow of their
affectionate mother. She had no apparent prejudice on the subject,

but had been told that her dear children were in danger of being drowned, the water in some parts of the river being deep. She was weak enough to believe this, and alluded to it in her conversation with me with much apprehension, but with no feeling of prejudice or unkindness. The poor father had also threatened to be present and hinder them, but the Lord suffered him not.

Another of the candidates was the brother who had hitherto been the village favourite. He had some complaint in his eye which he was tempted to fear would be increased, but faith eventually got the better of his unbelief. A beloved brother came from Barnstaple to preach the gospel, and as we walked together and conversed on our way to the river, the Lord graciously dispelled all my previous fears.

A large multitude assembled to witness the strange sight, and the ministry of the word was with power, so that not the slightest disorder was permitted to disturb the solemnity of the scene. A body of unruly men had gathered on the opposite side of the river, having come from Chittlehamholt with the avowed intention of annoying us, but they were overawed and restrained by an invisible power. One of these, E. M—— said afterwards, "we on our side meant to have begun when the dipping went on, but somehow or other we couldn't do it." This man subsequently became a subject of divine grace, and some time before his conversion he saw me baptise his wife in the same river; he has now for many years been with Christ.

The aged mother who accompanied her beloved daughters with such an anxious mind was herself destined to share in the blessings of that day. The cottage[6] in which we changed our dress was half a mile from the river, and when I met her there after the baptism she was in tears, and at first I attributed them to the joy she experienced at the safety of those so dear to her. But it was soon evident that there was another and a deeper cause. Whether they were tears

---

6 The same letter which informed me a few days since of the happy departure of Rachel to be with the Lord, contained also the cheering news that J. N—— who occupied the cottage at this time, has just been converted, and is now rejoicing in the Lord. He was called at the eleventh hour, being more than eighty years of age.

of sorrow for sin, or of joy at finding peace, I know not; perhaps both might have caused them to flow. It is however certain that the season proved to be a time of life to her soul, and from that time she became a faithful witness for the truth, enduring persecution of the most painful character with great submission, and commending the gospel by her testimony. When she was herself afterwards baptised, her unfeeling husband used the horse-whip on her return home without her uttering a word of complaint. While suffering as a Christian she was not ashamed, but was enabled to glorify God on this behalf. (See 1 Peter 4:14-16)

> How lost was our condition
>   Till Jesus made us whole;
> There is but one Physician
>   Can cure a sin-sick soul.

> In sin and death he found us,
>   He snatched us from the grave
> To tell to all around us
>   His wondrous power to save,

CHAPTER XXI

THE CHAPEL

"My God shall supply all your need according to His
riches in glory by Christ Jesus."—Philippians 4:19

THE room in which our meetings were held during the
winter was merely a back cellar, with but little light, and
much too small to accommodate the hearers; so that a more
convenient building seemed indispensable. My first step about this
matter was taken in January, 1884, when a short statement of our
need was printed, and circulated among some Christian friends. My
reasons for adopting this plan were thus stated:—

1st. Because it is desired that this chapel may be erected by the
free will contributions of the Lord's people.
2nd. Because it is not considered scriptural to leave important
labours in the gospel to solicit subscriptions in person.
3rd. Because the whole amount now given will be *devoted to its
proper object,* and no part expended in travelling expenses.[7]

---

7 I have sometimes ministered in a chapel which was burthened with debt,
and was told that a former minister once travelled some distance to solicit help
to discharge it. He was, however, so unsuccessful that on his return he tried to
make a charge on the congregation for part of his journeying expenses, which he
had not collected money enough to defray.

It was also stated that no debt would be contracted, nor the work begun, until sufficient subscriptions had been received to complete the walls and roof of the intended building.

The common practice of erecting chapels with borrowed money appeared to me very unscriptural. If I had faith to trust the Lord for my own support, it must surely be wrong to mistrust Him for anything needful for the promotion of His glory in the salvation of souls. I am fully aware that debts of this kind are not only justified, but considered by some to be necessary, as furnishing a plea for appealing to the liberality of what is termed "the Christian public." But surely this is miserable sophistry, and a libel on the church of God.

I determined therefore to leave the matter in the Lord's hand, and build only as He sent supplies; and my confidence in Him was amply rewarded. Almost the first donation was from a clergyman who heard me preach in the open air near his house, and remained in conversation with me some time after. Twenty pounds were next sent from the late Sir J. K——, whom I never saw, or corresponded with; and twenty more was given by another Christian of the Independent denomination, who told me that he considered it an honour to support such a work. Indeed the supplies came in much faster than I had anticipated, according to the grace of Him who is able to do for us "exceeding abundantly above all we ask or think." Ephesians 3:20. Within a few weeks one half of the hundred and fifty pounds required for the building was sent to me. It may be thought by some that this was owing to the *printed statement* of the case, but *if this only* was needed, or *believed* to be so, the plan would be universally adopted. I then regarded it, and still do so, as the Lord's gracious approval of our dependence on Him for all we needed. If we had grace more entirely to honour Him by leaving Him to do His own work in His own way, very many of the difficulties we now labour under would soon vanish.

When I erected a fourth chapel ten years afterwards *no* statement was *printed,* but the same plan was, in other respects, followed. On that occasion I received a twenty pound bank note from an individual whose name was not familiar to me, nor should I have recollected it, if he had not reminded me in his letter that we once met when he was making a morning call at Clifton; and about the same time there came another letter containing twenty-five pounds from two Christians, both of them entirely unknown to me. In each case the chapels were completed within six or seven months.

An interesting circumstance which proved the Lord's watchful care over us, in meeting all our need, occurred at this time. When the chapel was nearly completed, our funds were exhausted, and for about a fortnight the work ceased. Just at this time a small party of Christian friends came to see me. One of them was a Christian brother of ample means, whom I had not before known, and who had come from Ireland to visit that neighbourhood. They remained at our prayer meeting, where the prayers of the young converts especially interested the brother alluded to, and a few days after his return he sent ten pounds towards the building, which was just about the sum we required to complete it.

The chapel at Chittlehamholt was built after I ceased to labour there, but the same plan was not adopted, and the result was what might have been expected; debt was contracted, which caused much anxiety. It was, some time afterwards, liquidated through the Lord's abounding grace.

The three youths whose conversion has been stated to have occurred nearly at the same time, were baptised early in the morning of the day when the chapel was first used for worship. One of them was greatly opposed by his father, who was a very depraved character. As the dear youth escaped from home by stealth, he was pursued, met on the road, and beaten. Not being permitted to return to his father's house after his baptism, it was my privilege to shelter and support him for a time. He was thus early made to know persecution for the truth's sake; after some weeks however, shame constrained the poor father to receive him again under his roof. T. K—— has now for many years been entirely engaged in the work of the ministry, in which I have been informed that the Lord has greatly blessed him.

CHAPTER XXII

THE CONSUMPTIVE

"Thou changest his countenance, and
sendest him away."—Job 14:20

IT will be remembered that I once ministered at the village of
Langridge Ford, when on my way to High Bickington, and was
kindly entertained by a poor woman, who with her two daughters,
were afterwards converted. These, together with some others residing in that place, were baptised in the autumn of 1837. Among that
number was J. M——, who, though married, was young in years,
and who had scarcely known the power of the truth, when he sick-
ened beneath deeply rooted disease. Consumption in his case made
rapid progress, as did also the grace of God in his soul. I have seldom
beheld a countenance beaming with brighter joy than he exhibited
whenever I met him; a joy which seemed to raise him above all his
pain and weariness. He appeared by his whole conduct and conversation to say, "to me to live in Christ and to die is gain." Philippians
1:21. Nor did I ever perceive in him any of that depression which is so
commonly connected with the malady that was fast hastening him to
the grave. When he heard of the intended baptism, he immediately
desired to unite with his fellow Christians in the public confession of
the Lord Jesus. Being assured that his remaining days were very few,
and knowing that this testimony to the truth was much despised by

the neighbouring population, I tried to dissuade him from his purpose, fearing that should he be suddenly removed after being baptised, reproach would thereby be cast upon the gospel. This fear doubtlessly resulted from unbelief, to which we are in many ways so prone, and I have reason to be thankful that the simplicity of this dear brother's faith was used by the Lord to constrain me to fulfil his desire, which I felt at length bound to do, when every argument failed to change his determination. As soon as I expressed this, he exclaimed with a joyful countenance, "Now I desire nothing for this world beyond strength for that day." This, his last request, was granted to such an extent that his highest anticipations were more than realized, and all fears respecting the issue were dispelled through the manifest power and grace of Him in whom he trusted. When I called at his cottage on the evening previous to his baptism, he was seated by the fire in profuse perspiration, with much cough, and apparently scarcely able to walk across the room. But his purpose was unchanged, and as the river was three miles distant over a hilly road, his friends had engaged a donkey and cart to convey him thither. The next morning when he arose, he felt no better; but as the hour for leaving drew nigh, he suddenly rallied, and seemed as one endowed with supernatural strength. He refused the conveyance which had been provided, and walked to the river with an energy and vigour that surprised all who saw him, and when I met him there it was difficult to believe that he was the same person I had seen in so much weakness the preceding evening. As the river was shallow we had to walk some way in, and while doing this he looked back to the numerous spectators on the shore, and said with a smile, "Deny thyself, and take up thy cross and follow me."

It had been arranged for him to be the last baptised, that he might go at once to the nearest cottage and change; but he refused to leave until the service was quite ended, and when we sung the Doxology, in which he heartily joined, he commenced the repetition of the two last lines.

He was filled with joy at being thus permitted to confess his Lord ere he quitted this sorrowing world, and remarked to me while dressing, "Now I don't care how I am tomorrow." He was satisfied at having borne testimony to the death and resurrection of Him who had given him a hope full of immortality. After his baptism instead of at once returning home he accompanied us to High Bickington, where the remainder of the day was spent in worship and communion. He had walked altogether on that day about seven miles, *without having once coughed;* and it was cause for especial thankfulness, that he not only sustained no injury but was for some time in better health than before, so that no one was heard to say that his death had been hastened by his confession of the name of Him whom his soul loved.

His life was prolonged about four months, when he peacefully fell asleep in Jesus. I ministered in his cottage the evening before his death from Colossians 3:4, and the door of the staircase was left open at his request, so that he was enabled to hear the blessed tidings of the gospel to almost his last hour on earth. Ere the morning dawned he was with Christ.

The interest excited by his peculiar case was so great that on the day of his burial many were unable to get within the walls of the chapel. I addressed the assembled company on that occasion by commenting on Proverbs 14:32.

This brief account of J. M—— may teach us that *true* happiness is independent of all circumstances; and that while the vain delights of this shadowy world are utterly incapable of affording lasting joy, the soul that realises peace with God is truly happy, and prepared for every event that can befall it. The wonderful display of the Lord's grace also in reference to the baptism of this dear brother, may remind us of the promise that to those who delight themselves in the Lord, He will give the desire of their hearts. Psalm 37:4.

> "Brother! thou hast passed the bourne
> Of this world of sin and woe;
> Now thou wilt no longer mourn,
> Nor a single tear-drop flow.

Higher praises now are thine,
    Than e'er flowed from mortal tongue;
We had nothing so divine,
    In the sweetest hymns we sung.

When we think of joy like this,
    We would fain be gone like thee;
Leave this world, and rise to bliss,
    And to immortality,"

CHAPTER XXIII

REMOVAL

"I will instruct thee and teach thee in the way
which thou shalt go."—Psalm 32:8

AFTER a residence of six years in High Bickington my mind
became exercised about removal. I was not able to account
for this feeling, being truly happy in my intercourse with
the dear saints, to whom also my service was acceptable. But I
have since clearly seen it to be *of the Lord,* whose purpose it was to
lead me elsewhere, to break up the fallow ground in some places
where the gospel was little known. I had hitherto fallen in with
the common impression that every minister of God's truth was
a pastor, and the distinctive character of the gifts bestowed on
different individuals "according to the grace given to us" had not
occupied my mind. But I now began to wonder that such passages
as Romans 12:6-9; Ephesians 4:11-12, and others of a similar character, had been so long unnoticed; and felt for the first time that
while others might be endowed by the Lord with different gifts for
watching over and feeding the flock, my own service for the Lord
was simply that of an evangelist. With this impression I desired
the dear saints no longer to consider me as their "pastor," though
I should be most anxious to seek their welfare, and to exercise
such oversight as the Lord might enable me as long as I remained

among them; but I had a decided impression that this would only be for a short time, as the event proved.

I was the more confirmed in this opinion as R. P—— one of the young brethren baptised September, 1884, had for some time been accustomed to minister, and there were evident tokens that the Lord had called him to the work of edifying the saints; so that there would be no lack of the ministry of the word by one who had their full confidence, and who was beloved by them for his work's sake. At this time there were about thirty meeting in communion; many others who had been converted had either left the village or had been taken to be with the Lord. A still larger number had been gathered at Chittlehamholt, Where the saints were under the oversight of a dear servant of the Lord, who had gone to reside with them after W. C——'s departure, and his labours had been owned to their souls' blessing.

On New Year s Day, 1889, I met a very happy company of believers at Coleridge for Christian intercourse and communion; and was invited by a brother in the Lord to spend a few days with him at North Tawton, a town four miles distant, which I did soon afterwards.. A day or two after my arrival he asked me to go with him to the village of Coleford, seven miles off, where a meeting for reading the scriptures was held every Wednesday afternoon. The thought of such a meeting at such a time much interested me and I willingly accompanied him. About half way on the road lay the village of Bow, where I was told a Home Missionary had laboured many years, but had lately, been withdrawn. An impression came almost instantly on my mind that this might be the place appointed for my future residence, and my subsequent meeting with about twenty persons to read the scriptures at Coleford at such an unusual hour, seemed to confirm my expectation that a work of God was about to be accomplished in that neighbourhood. It also appeared providential that there was a vacant cottage at Bow which was likely to suit me. If I have dwelt much on the particulars of this journey it is on account of its results, as being connected with much useful labour during the next seven years, and as showing by what comparatively trivial circumstances the Lord may sometimes make known His will to those who wait on Him, and desire in all things to be guided by His counsel.

On my return home the dear saints were greatly distressed when informed that I might probably soon leave them, and it caused me no little sorrow that they all thought that by doing so I should be acting contrary to the mind of the Lord. I should have trembled to do this, and was deeply exercised in mind because their judgment was so contrary to my own in this matter; but I was led thereby more unceasingly to cast it upon the Lord, and to seek his direction alone; and where the heart is upright His guidance is sure. The result was that the conviction of my own mind became deepened. I felt bound to follow in the path which I believed the Lord had appointed me, and about the middle of March I removed to Bow, having met the dear saints at a parting tea meeting the previous evening.

As I may not again allude to the place just quitted, it affords me much joy to state that during an absence of seventeen years, the work of God has continued to prosper, both as regards the growth of the dear saints in knowledge, and the increase of their faith and love. Many souls have also been gathered to Christ through the ministry of the gospel by the dear brother already alluded to — the bereaved husband of Rachel — who in addition to his public services, has watched over the saints with a truly pastoral care, seeking no reward of his labour save that which he will receive at the hands of the chief shepherd "the crown of glory that fadeth not away." 1 Peter 5:4 Often has my; heart been cheered by tidings of their welfare, and it was my privilege not long ago to visit them, and to witness "their order and the stedfastness of their faith in Christ." This little band of saints has truly been "a light shining in a dark place."

"I thank my God upon every remembrance of you, always in every prayer of mine for you all making request with joy, for your fellowship in the gospel from the first day until now." Philippians 1:3-5.

CHAPTER XXIV

A SECOND HARVEST SEASON

"Believers were the more added to the Lord."— Acts 5:14

I CAME to reside at Bow in March, 1889. For some time there was much that seemed to give me encouragement, but my expectations were soon disappointed through the falling away of many of whom I had hoped well. My stay in that place was not, however, altogether in vain, as there were a few decided conversions; and if my hopes were not fully realised there, they were abundantly so in the neighbourhood around. For the first few months my labours were mostly confined to Bow and Coleford; and in the following year I went to reside in a more central situation, it being evident that the latter place was that which needed most of my time, and that much desire for the gospel was beginning to be manifested in some other places around it.

W. P——, a poor man aged seventy, and who had kindly offered his cottage for the ministry of the gospel at Coleford, was the first to receive it as "glad tidings of great joy." While preaching there the third or fourth time I observed tears fast flowing down his cheeks; and they proved to be tears of repentance and godly sorrow, which were soon after exchanged for the joy of God's salvation. He lived for about ten years after to be a witness to the truth, bringing forth fruit in his old age. His daughter and her husband, who lived in the same cottage, were soon after made partakers of the same grace. My heart was greatly comforted and cheered by this early manifestation of the Lord's presence with me in a fresh field of labour in the gospel* Several other conversions followed during the summer of this year, and it became evident that the Lord had many souls to bring to the knowledge of His truth. In the establishment of a wealthy farmer, several labourers and some of their wives were made the subjects of divine grace. T. H——, the waggoner, was at first greatly opposed to the gospel, and his enmity was especially excited by the conversion of his fellow servant, who lived in the next cottage; and also by his own wife being awakened to feel her need of salvation. His boisterous and quarrelsome temper was a great trial to the other workmen on the farm, and it was increasingly manifested when he beheld the work of the Lord around him. It was truly seen in him that "the carnal mind is enmity against God, for it is not subject to the law of God, neither indeed can be." Romans 8:7. But the Lord was about to manifest his power and grace in subduing this enmity, and bringing him to the cross of Jesus.

It was on the evening of a stormy day, that after labouring at the plough he returned home drenched with rain, and to the great surprise of his wife told her he was going to hear the preaching. Being an old man and subject to infirmities, his wife, who at any other time would have encouraged him, was fearful of the results and begged him to remain home. But all her remonstrances were in vain, his purpose was fixed, and the result made manifest that in this he was directed by the Lord, who used the occasion for his conversion. From that time he was a changed man, and his whole conduct gave evidence of the reality of the Lord's work in his soul. His wife also soon after found peace, and both have now for some years been with Christ. Another labourer on the same farm, who had previously known the Lord but had much declined in spirit, was blessed through the ministry, and was not only restored to health-fulness of soul, but became useful also in the ministry of the word to others. The Lord blessed his testimony to the conversion, of some sinners. This change in him excited much interest among his former associates, especially as he had been formerly noted for bell-ringing, dancing, and all the jollities of village life; sometimes spending the whole night in dissipation, and going from it to commence the next day's labour. He has now continued to serve God in the gospel of His Son for seventeen years.

Another instance of the power of the truth was seen in the parish clerk. He had long been converted, but now began to see that he could not conscientiously retain his office, and he willingly gave up its emoluments and helped in the ministry of the word, for which the Lord had well qualified him. The two villages of Bow and Coleford were thus regularly supplied. In other places also there was soon a call for the gospel, which rendered this help needful.

Among other conversions were some of the domestics of a gentleman, who was a Magistrate residing in the immediate vicinity, and favourable to the gospel. When they with some others were about to be baptised, the enmity of many who were lovers of pleasure more than lovers of God, was greatly excited, as the groom, one of the number, had hitherto been one of their boon companions at the alehouse. I have never on any similar occasion seen that enmity so openly exhibited. One of the publicans sons was the chief instigator of the disturbance, My soul was deeply exercised during this solemn season. I felt some small degree of liberty while in prayer, but when I attempted to address the spectators I was quite powerless, and after a few observations felt it was in vain to proceed. Among the crowd was a man who came with the avowed intention to mock this sacred ordinance, though entreated by his wife,

SCRIPTURE TESTIMONY
Holy Spirit convicts people of their sin
JOHN 16:8

who knew something of the power of truth, not to do so. But the Lord met with him in the way, and exhibited the power of His grace in subduing the enmity of his heart, and making him willing to follow Jesus. It is remarkable that the few words which I felt to be so powerless were those to which he attributed his conversion. On the following Lord's day he purposely came to meet me in the road, and to tell me what the Lord had done for his soul, and he soon after made an open profession of faith in Christ, by being himself baptised in His name.

CHAPTER XXV

A CRY FOR THE GOSPEL

"Come over and help us." Acts 16:9

PREVIOUS to my coming into the neighbourhood a rich farmer, who lived at Woodland Head four miles from Coleford, had requested a minister of the gospel to come and preach near his house. He was himself an infidel, and led a very immoral life, glorying in his shame, but the dishonesty of his workmen was his reason for this singular application. He did not care whether they were taught Christianity, or Popery, or Mahommedanism, but foolishly imagined that instruction of any kind would improve their character. I need scarcely add that his wish was not responded to.

About the close of the summer a woman, who had heard of the entrance of the gospel into Coleford, sent a request that it might be brought into her neighbourhood, and offered her cottage for ministry. She was a tenant of the farmer just mentioned, and lived about a mile from

SCRIPTURE TESTIMONY
Unbelievers pleading to hear the Gospel
ACTS 16:9-10
A person God has prepared to hear the Gospel
MATTHEW 10:13 · LUKE 10:6

his house. This application seemed to come as from the Lord, and her desire was granted. I first went there on a stormy evening in October, and after passing over seven miles of rough and hilly road, came to two cottages, no others being within some distance. Everything to outward appearance was bleak and cheerless, but the sight of about forty persons gathered in such a place, and in such weather, to hear the word of life, greatly cheered me, and seemed indicative of future blessing. There was no church or other place for public worship within two or three miles, and the inhabitants generally were totally ignorant and depraved. Here, as at Coleford, the person who received the gospel into her house, was the first to realise its power in her own soul.[8]

While I was once taking tea with her previous to the service we conversed about faith, and I endeavoured to show from the word, the simplicity of the act by which we receive salvation, although all the power is of God. The Holy Spirit applied this truth so directly and powerfully to her soul,, that while listening she said to herself, "I *believe* it, and *know* I am *saved for ever.*" She did not inform me of this for a year or two after, but the change wrought in her was speedily manifested. I had frequent opportunities of observing that in this place, where the gospel had not before been heard, the tidings of God's mercy through Christ, as promised freely to all who believe in him, were received with a simplicity that I had not witnessed elsewhere.[9] Through the whole of the winter, the good seed of the

---

8   These are only some of the many instances in which the truth has been blessed to those who willingly opened their houses for the ministry of the word. I have always been unwilling to go where *rent* was expected for such a purpose. "If the house be *worthy,* let your peace come upon it, but if it be not worthy, let your peace return to you." Matthew 10:13

9   I have on different occasions met with believers who seemed to doubt the reality of such sudden conversions as have been frequently mentioned in these "Recollections," and it may be well to observe that I have not described any distinct case except where it has been proved to be the work of the Holy Spirit after years of subsequent observation.

Such doubts often arise from a mistaken idea that conversion must be a *gradual,* instead of an *instantaneous* work; there can however be no period between life and death in a material body, and the analogy is strictly applicable to a sinner "dead in trespasses and sins," Ephesians 2:1, when quickened by

word was taking root in many hearts, and in the following summer the fruit began to gladden my eyes abundantly. Some of the cases were of a very interesting character, among which were those of two boys, J. H—— and W. G——, of the ages of sixteen and fourteen. They were waiting on the outside of the cottage one evening, and H——, the elder boy, offered to take my horse. Being interested in his appearance I asked him why he did this, and added, "Do you love Jesus?" "Yes, sir." How do you *know* you love him?" "Be cause he has pardoned my sins." *"How long* have you known this?" "Ever since Monday"—it was now Wednesday. I afterwards learned that he had been awakened under the word the week previous, and found peace on Monday. He added, "Besides, those who don't love Jesus make God a liar." "Can you read?" "No, sir." I was so much astonished, I could scarcely believe what I had heard, which I have recorded word for word as it was spoken. Looking at the younger boy, I said "And what of that boy?" "Oh! he says he'll try for't too." To some this may seem a mere childish incident, but I have never since had a moment's reason to doubt that a work of grace was at this time commenced in their souls. The youngest of these was baptised about three months after, and his whole conduct since that time has been most consistent. The eldest was baptised the year following. Both of them formed part of the family of a farmer who was greatly opposed to the truth, but was destined to witness much of its power among the labourers who worked on his estate. Two months after the conversion of these dear youths, I baptised for the first time in that neighbourhood, and a young man from the same family came to witness the scene, which was at the early hour of seven in the morning. He brought with him a large sheep dog, saying "We will baptise the dog first," but through the ministry of

---

the Holy Spirit. "He that believeth on the Son *hath* everlasting life" John 3:36. So also John 5:24, "passed from death unto life." A dear Christian, who once expressed her doubts about such conversions as I have described, asked me some years after how the converts went on; and on being told that they were walking happily in the Lord's ways, she said with a sigh, "then I don't know whether I have any faith at all."

the word on *that same day,* by a brother from Coleford, this young scoffer was made to feel the power of the truth, and became himself a follower of the Lord Jesus. About ten of the labourers and their families who worked on that farm, were brought to the knowledge of the truth within about one year from the commencement of ministry in the cottage, besides many others. Their master greatly opposed them, but could not shake their faith. He once came to hear the ministry, and afterwards greatly exposed his ignorance, by endeavouring to show that I contradicted myself in different parts of the discourse, but did not come again. After some years he was constrained to decline all opposition. He had seen so much to commend in the conduct of his men, that he at last informed them he should no longer endeavour to hinder their following the dictates of their consciences.

There were also many other conversions to which I had not yet alluded, two of which will form the subjects of the next chapters. The power of the gospel was especially seen in several young men, besides those already mentioned, whose conduct greatly commended the truth as it is in Jesus.

In no previous year had I so much joy in reference to the progress of the gospel, as in 1840. There was abundant cause for thanksgiving both at Coleford and Woodland Head, and some also at Bow, although the latter proved to be a place of trial and disappointment. For some time all the converts came to the Lord's table at Coleford, where there was much difficulty in procuring a place for meeting. Our need was only supplied at length by renting a stable, on which a somewhat large sum had to be expended ere it could be used for worship. The small band of communicants, which at first consisted of only ten persons, increased to nearly eighty within one year and a half, and the number of persons baptised in and near the three villages in this year, was fifty-seven.

The evident change seen in the conduct of many persons excited much interest in the neighbourhood, so that some came from a distance of six, and even eight miles, to hear the gospel, or to commune with us at the table of the Lord. One of these, who had formerly met with Wesleyans, earnestly desired to have ministry in his house at Tedburn, being four miles beyond Woodland Head, and eight from Coleford. At this time another helper had joined us in the work, so that we were enabled to supply this fresh demand, the Lord meeting our need as we went along. This dear brother, who was one of the gardeners of the Christian magistrate already mentioned, with two other helpers, now went the several distances of four or eight miles every Lord's day to proclaim the glad tidings of salvation. At Tedburn also, as at the other places, the power of the truth was first experienced in the house where it was willingly received, the wife of the brother at whose request it was brought there being converted very soon after. Here also many witnesses were raised up to testify the truth of the gospel, and a company of beloved saints continue to worship there to this day.

> "What is our hope, or joy, or crown of rejoicing?
> Are not even ye in the presence of our Lord
> Jesus Christ at his coming? For ye are our
> glory and joy." 1 Thessalonians 2:19-20

CHAPTER XXVI

THE PRAYING WIFE

"If we ask any thing according to His
will He heareth us."—1 John 5:14

GREAT are the triumphs of faith as recorded in Hebrews 11:34, in reference to the saints of former days. They "obtained promises," Genesis 21:1-2; "Stopped the mouths of lions," Daniel 6:22; "Quenched the violence of fire," Daniel 3:27; "Women received their dead raised to life," 2 Kings 4:32-85, &c. When the centurion heard his daughter was dead, and was hidden "not to trouble the Master any further," the consoling answer of Jesus was, "Be not afraid, *only* believe," Mark 5:36; and His word of promise to His people still is, "All things, whatsoever ye shall ask in prayer *believing,* ye shall receive," Matthew 21:22. If in these days of weakness but little of the power of faith is manifested, there are yet some of God's dear children who know that it is a reality by the answers they receive to their prayers. I was led to these observations by remembering the following circumstance.

A lady who was accustomed to visit some cottages near her own house, was once praying with some poor women with whom she sometimes met to read the scriptures, and while thus engaged, A. F——, from Woodland Head, came in, and was so astonished, that she afterwards enquired what the lady had been doing. This led to some conversation with the lady herself, to whom she acknowledged her ignorance, telling her there was no preaching in their neighbourhood and they knew nothing. She was told she ought to pray to the Lord to send His gospel to them through some of His servants. This occurred not long before it was actually sent to within about a mile of her cottage, and the Lord had prepared her heart to receive it. Among the many converts at that place there was none who more commended the gospel by exhibiting its transforming power in her *whole* conduct; the result of a deep experience of it in her own soul.

SCRIPTURE TESTIMONY
Pray for all people, that they may come to Christ
1 TIMOTHY 2:1-4

She was baptised, with several others, in the autumn of 1840, when George, her husband was present without exhibiting any sign of disapprobation. But on their way home he became very angry, and assailed her with bitter words, Anne remained silent during the outburst of his passion, but like Hannah of old, she "spake in her heart," and out of the abundance of her grief "poured out her soul to the Lord." 1 Samuel 1:15-16. She was not faithless, but believing, and boldly asked the Lord to *convert him within a week.* Perhaps she remembered the word, "Is anything too hard for the Lord?" Genesis 18:14. At all events it was the prayer of faith, and the Lord heard and answered it. On the following day George was still morose and angry, and although his work lay not far from his cottage he took his dinner with him to the field. It was a time of temptation, and when about noon his anger had reached its height he said to himself, "I will go home and tear her to pieces." But his wife's prayer had been heard in heaven, and the answer was about to be granted. He went home and told her his purpose was to kill her. She wept, not on her own account, as she told him, but because of the hardness of his heart. Strange to relate, the lion was in an instant changed into a lamb. George, too, began to weep, and asked if such a vile sinner as he was could be saved. The result may be anticipated. This was the period of his spiritual birth. If such a change as that of which he was now the subject had been foretold twenty-four hours previously, many would have replied, "If the Lord would make windows in heaven might this thing be?" 2 Kings 7:2 But the Lord in the operations of His grace mocks our feeble calculations, and acts according to His own sovereign will and purpose, "putting down the mighty from their seats, and exalting them of low degree." Luke 1:52

When on my way to their cottage on the following morning, I heard George's voice calling to me from a neighbouring field, and heard from his own lips how wonderfully the Lord had dealt with him. His whole future life proved the reality of the change so suddenly wrought in his soul. He was afflicted with an asthmatic complaint which often laid him aside from work for weeks together, and he was never well enough to earn full wages. His poverty was on this account very deep, and I have scarcely ever known a case which more demanded sympathy; but on no occasion did I ever hear from his lips or those of his dear wife a word of murmuring or complaint. I saw him about three years ago, at the close of a day in which he had been trying to help in the harvest field. His bodily weakness was great, but his heart was full, and all he could do was to hold one of my hands in his and say, "Dear Mr. G——, dear Mr. G——," while his eyes streamed with tears. His earthly course was at this time nearly finished, and early in the following year, 1855, he peacefully departed to be with Him whom his soul loved.

> Ended thy pilgrimage with all its ills.
> Thy shattered body hath a quiet home;
> The spirit, free and disencumbered, dwells
> Where night and weariness can never come.

> Thine is the peaceful portion of the blest,
> No longer by the storms of sorrow driven;
> Safe in the mighty Saviour's arms at rest,
> Amid th'eternal melodies of heaven.

Much might be said of his dear wife, as of one who loved the Lord above many. The sphere of her testimony was very limited, but she did what she could, and sought to adorn the gospel in all things. She was deeply anxious for the spiritual welfare of her children, and they were the constant subject of her prayers. In spite of deep poverty it was many months ere she consented to send her eldest daughter to reside with some relations in London, (who promised to care for her), lest by too much haste she might act contrary to the Lords will, and her child thereby suffer loss. On one occasion I was most unexpectedly presented with a sovereign for the use of this dear family, and it reached them at a very interesting time. When on my way to their cottage I was told that Anne was in great trouble. Her two boys, on account of their parent's poverty, had hitherto been instructed at the parish school gratuitously, but she had now been told that this favour could not be continued unless they were sent to the church Sunday-school. This was a sore trial of her faith, as they had hitherto been instructed on the Lord's day by some brethren who met for worship in the cottage, and she was very unwilling to remove them, but she determined not to consent until she had seen me. On my coming to see her just at this time and hearing her tale of sorrow, I asked her if she could not trust the Lord for fourpence a week? She replied, "I know I ought to, but poverty is a great temptation." On my again asking what she would say if she knew I had money enough with me to pay for their schooling for more than twelve months, she added, "Then I must praise the Lord and shame the devil,"

(I feel sure she did not mean to use this expression in an irreverent sense. She felt she had been tempted to doubt the Lord's goodness on this occasion, and perhaps remembered James 4:7)

When she once applied for the gift money annually distributed to the poor of her parish, it was at first refused by the magistrate on the ground of her being able to support the preaching on which she attended. On her saying she paid nothing, it was asked "What! no preachers horse-hire?" "No, sir, it is all free cost." "What do they preach then?" "They don't preach at all, sir." "Not preach at all! What do they do, then?" "They explain the word of God sir."

"Settle it therefore in your hearts, not to meditate before what ye shall answer. For I will give you a mouth and wisdom which all your adversaries shall not be able to gainsay or resist."—Luke 21:14-15

There is an eye that never sleeps
    Beneath the wing of night;
There is an ear that never shuts,
    When sinks the beams of light.

There is an arm that never tires,
    When human strength gives way;
There is a love that never fails,
    When earthly loves decay.

That eye is fixed on seraph throngs;
    That arm uplifts the sky;
That ear is fixed on angel songs;
    That love is throned on high.

But there's a power which man can wield,
    When mortal aid is vain,
That eye, that arm, that love to reach,
    That listening ear to gain.

That power is prayer, which soars on high,
    Through Jesus, to the throne;
And moves the hand that moves the world,
    To bring salvation down.

CHAPTER XXVII

THE GREAT DEBTOR

"By grace are ye saved, through faith, and that not
of yourselves, it is the gift of God; not of works
lest any man should boast."—Ephesians 2:8-9.

I T is interesting and profitable to observe the various ways by
which the Lord is pleased to call sinners to Himself. In the last
chapter we have seen one who like Paul was "breathing out
threatenings and slaughter" suddenly brought to the feet of Jesus
in the one preceding the last is the account of a poor boy converted
through ministry, and soon brought into liberty, and his younger
companion attracted and led to Christ solely by his example. In the
third chapter, the text of a sermon is used, and I once remember the
last verse of a hymn read before the sermon, having been blessed
also to the same end. We are now to see an aged sinner, without any
previous instrumentality, quickened by the Holy Ghost, when in
the immediate prospect of death. Truly the Lord giveth no account
of His matters, but says to us all "My counsel shall stand, and I will
do all my pleasure." Isaiah 46:10.

At the close of the same summer, 1840, I heard that W. M——was
ill and likely to die. He was one of the workmen of the infidel farmer
alluded to in Chapter XXV; a profane man, and advanced in years.
He had not, to my knowledge, attended the ministry of the gospel

which for ten months had been preached near his house. He had joined with others in reaping the fruits of the earth, and was himself soon to be cut down by the scythe of the great mower, *death*. It was evident at my first visit that his remaining days would be few, and to my great joy it was soon manifest that the Spirit of God was working in his soul. He was deeply convinced of sin, and feared the infliction of its awful penalty. He knew that "the wages of sin is death," but as yet he knew not that "the gift of God is eternal life." Romans 6:23.

> **SCRIPTURE TESTIMONY**
>
> *Jesus is able to save
> to the uttermost*
>
> HEBREWS 7:25

The state of his mind was evident from the following brief conversation, which is too deeply impressed on my memory to be forgotten.

M. "If I owed you a thousand pounds, you would put me to prison, would'nt you?" On my replying in the negative, he said—

M. "But if I *did* owe you the money, and you *did* put me to prison, I must stay there till the debt was paid, and I could say nothing against it."

I now understood his meaning, and said if he meant to refer to his state as a sinner before God it was all true—that it was not the "thousand pounds," but the "ten thousand talents," Matthew 18:24, that every sin he had committed, and every idle word he had spoken, stood as a debt against him— that he could not pay one farthing of it— yet if it was not paid, he must go to the prison of hell. After a pause, I said, "but I can tell you of some one who will pay it for you." On his asking what I meant I referred him to *Christ,* when he said

M. "Christ wont do that for me. I am *too great* a sinner."

I cannot describe my joy at this confession. It seemed as though I saw him already at the feet of Jesus. He needed not the thunders of Sinai to awaken him. The wound was open, and he wanted only the healing balm. The two portions of scripture to which I especially referred him, and on which I enlarged, were "the blood of Jesus Christ cleanseth us from all sin," 1 John 1:7, and "He is able to save unto the uttermost them that come unto God by Him;" Hebrews 7:25, and after praying with him I went home full of confidence and hope, which was soon happily realised.

On my way to his cottage two days after, I was informed that W. M——— had found peace. The news had already been spread around. His first words on seeing me enter his cottage were "Oh, sir! I can die now "—and on my asking what he meant, he said, "My burden is gone, Jesus has pardoned my sins," and it was indeed true; he had believed God's testimony concerning Him who died for the sins of many, and "being justified by faith, he had peace with God through our Lord Jesus Christ," Romans 5:1

His life was prolonged a few weeks after this, and in all my subsequent visits I found him happily resting on the Lord until taken to be with him for ever.

Of the various cases of conversion which it has been my privilege to witness, there is not one which more distinctly sets forth the great principles of the gospel than that of this "poor debtor."

1st.   He *felt* himself to be what he really was, and what we are *all* by nature—a *great sinner*. Romans 3:10-23.

2nd. Like the debtor in Matthew 18:25 and Luke 7:42, he knew he had "nothing to pay." He saw nothing in himself on which to ground any plea for mercy. The great hindrance to the reception of the "gospel which brings salvation," Titus 2:11, is the mistaken idea, arising from pride, or ignorance, or both, that we must bring something to God; not knowing that by nature we are "wretched, and miserable, and poor, and blind and naked." Revelation 3:17

3rd. He readily received the offer of free pardon through Christ, *believing* that he came into the world to save sinners, 1 Timothy 1:15, and also that "God so loved the world that He *gave* His only begotten Son, Jesus Christ, that *whosoever* believeth on Him should not perish, but have everlasting life." John 3:16.

4th. Through the reception of this truth he was able at once to say "I can die now—my burden is gone—Jesus has pardoned my sins."

O where shall rest be found?
  Rest for the weary soul;
'Twere vain the ocean's depths to sound.
  Or search to either pole.

The world can never give
  The bliss for which we sigh;
'Tis not the whole of life to live,
  Nor all of death to die.

Beyond this vale of tears,
  There is a life above,
Unsullied by the flight of years,
  And all that life is love.

There is a death whose pang
  Outlives the fleeting breath;
Oh, what eternal horrors hang
  Around that second death!

Lord God of truth and grace,
  Teach all that death to shun,
Lest they be banished from thy face,
  And utterly undone.

CHAPTER XXVIII

THE TWO CONVERTED HUSBANDS

"Whatsoever ye shall ask in prayer, believing,
ye shall receive."—Matthew 21:22

THE three preceding chapters relate to the work which resulted from "the cry for the gospel." That cry led to the establishment of ministry which is still continued in two different places; and there was yet another locality, into which the Lord was about to send the same glad tidings. I had been accustomed occasionally to visit a Christian woman who lived three miles from Coleford, in another direction, where the population was even more scattered than in either of the other places, there being no village in the whole locality, and scarcely more than two houses near each other in any part of it. H. K—— was a woman of true piety, combined with much energy of character and real concern for the advancement of divine truth. She often expressed her conviction that the Lord had many souls to convert in that neighbourhood, at a time when there appeared no ground to expect the fulfilment of her hopes. She alluded in a similar way to her husband, who had the oversight of the estates of the Christian magistrate before alluded to. Thomas was unlike his wife in most particulars, and to her deep sorrow, was much addicted to intemperance. Yet she was so confident in her expectation of his conversion that she once observed "the Lord is not going to convert *half* of me." At her request I sometimes preached there, but with little expectation of blessing till encouraged by the following circumstance. There was another believer in the same district on whom I sometimes called. Her cottage lay at the bottom of a deep wood, and while endeavouring to find my way there, I once missed the right path, and seeing a man at work not far from me, I asked if he could inform me where Mary B. lived. With a very shrewd expression of countenance he replied, "I should *think* I could." I concluded from this that he was her husband, which proved to be the case. Robert was a sober and moral man of his class, and so thrifty and diligent that he soon after rose from being a labourer to be a small farmer, occupying thirty or forty acres of the coarse land in that district. I remained with him in conversation a few minutes, and endeavoured to explain to him the nature of the faith which receives salvation as God's free gift through Christ; for he had told me that he had for two years been trying to make himself better. This short interview was used by the Lord to his immediate conversion, causing him to pray, as he afterwards informed me, in a way he had never done before, and when X again saw him not long after, there could be no doubt that he had "passed from death unto life," and during the many years that have since passed, his conduct has been that of a sincere and humble follower of Christ. From this time my hopes respecting this neighbourhood were much encouraged, and I was led to minister there more frequently. The prayers of Hannah R. for her husband were now about to be answered, to the joy of her heart. He too was converted soon after, through the ministry of one of the brethren from Coleford. The work of the Lord in this solitary neighbourhood now began to increase, and some other conversions took place. It was the wish of Thomas to be baptised not far from his own locality, that his testimony might be near the place which had hitherto been the scene of his sin and folly. For some time, however, there was hindrance owing to the scarcity of water. But having the oversight of the estates of his employer, he found at length, in one of them, a place which suited the purpose. It lay in the interior of a farm occupied by C. S——, who was a respectable moral character. He had never attended our ministry, but willingly consented to allow me to baptise on his farm,[10] especially as he well knew that his landlord felt an interest in our exertions for the spread of the gospel. Many spectators were gathered to witness Thomas K——, and seven others, baptised in the name of the Lord Jesus, when a dear minister of Christ preached an awakening sermon from 2 Peter 21-23. The kindness of the farmer in allowing us to change at his house, and use the refreshment we had brought with us, sufficiently indicated that he entertained no prejudice against the truth, and our short conversation with him gave some encouragement to hope for happy results, which will be related in the next chapter.

> "The father bruised his only son
> For us upon the tree;
> His death is our eternal life,
> Our glorious liberty.
>
> Love moved the father's hand to smite,
> Love moved the son to bear;
> How sweet oh Calvary to stand!
> The God of Love is there."

---

10 My frequent allusions to Baptism, have not arisen from a wish to make it unduly prominent, but it will be evident to the reader how often the Lord used that very solemn ordinance to the blessing of many; and that several interesting details of my narrative, spring from events connected with the baptism of believers.

CHAPTER XXIX

THE CONVERTED FARMER

"He is a chosen vessel unto me."—Acts 9:15

ABOUT three months after the first baptism on the farm of C. S—— several others were baptised there, and one of the happy results was a sure conviction that the farmer himself had become deeply concerned for the salvation of his own soul. From this time he attended all our meetings, and at no distant period, both he and his dear wife, (who was converted about the same time), made a similar confession of their faith in Christ. The conversion of this beloved brother in the Lord was an event which called for much thanksgiving, not merely as regarded himself, but also in reference to the advancement of the truth in a neighbourhood where he soon became a faithful preacher of the gospel; and he also sought to watch over the newly converted saints with a truly pastoral care.

It is at all times an interesting employment to trace the various dealings of the Lord in His providence, and especially in those things which relate to His own glory in the promotion of the gospel. In the present case there were several distinct steps, all closely connected and leading to one happy result.

1st.   My missing the path on my way to Mary B ——'s cottage, led to the conversion of her husband, which was followed by a more regular ministry in that neighbourhood.

129

2nd. That ministry was used by the Lord for the conversion of another husband, in answer to the especial prayer of his wife.

3rd. His desire to be baptised in his own locality led to the conversion of two others, who being thus brought under the ministry of the gospel, listened to it, believed, and were saved.

4th. A Pastor and Evangelist was raised up to be used in the Lord's work, in which he has been greatly blessed, and made a blessing to many souls.

It is thus that the Lord directs the paths of our feet, and makes them subservient to the purposes of His mercy, grace, and love.

Afterwards, when there became a sufficient number of believers to meet at the Lord's table as a separate body from those at Coleford, and a larger number of persons came to hear the gospel, it was considered needful to provide a more convenient place of meeting. It was towards the close of my service in that neighbourhood, when Hannah K—— who was a zealous and active person, ventured to state this need to her husband's master, and boldly requested a small piece of land, and also all that was required for the erection of a small chapel. When it is considered that this gentleman was himself from principle a member of the Establishment, and that he was also the lay proprietor of the tithes of the parish, such a request will appear not a little extraordinary. But she knew his liberal principles, and his sincere desire to further any object which he considered likely to promote the welfare of those around him. He had carefully observed the effects of the gospel in his bailiff and tenant, and also in others connected with his own household, and after some deliberation he generously consented to do all she desired. The ground for a chapel and burying place was soon allotted, and I was commissioned to superintend the erection of a neat building, of a size suitable for the purpose intended, and to apply to him for money as the work went on. Much joy was expressed by the dear saints at the tidings of this generous act, and the work was soon commenced. But joy and sorrow are sometimes not far distant from each other, and such was the case in reference to the intended building, which had made but little progress when I began to feel that my service in that neighbourhood was drawing to a close. Had this occurred a little sooner, all hopes of obtaining a chapel would have been in vain; and as it now was, the gentleman alluded to was exceedingly tried—I may perhaps say displeased—at the prospect of my removal, fearing that the work would decline and suffer, if one single arm of flesh did not remain to carry it on. He immediately declared his intention to proceed no further with the building, which the poor saints were themselves totally unable to go on with. The walls were only about four feet high, and although the timber had been provided, the labour and other materials would involve much expense. But as the spring advanced, their zeal and energy were most conspicuous and praiseworthy, and in many unexpected ways the Lord helped them. Small contributions were given in money by some; others gave a few days labour, and all did their utmost, and that so heartily, that the gentleman, who observed all their movements, was heard to say, that if *he* had done the *whole* work, it would have been spoiled. I was also informed that he was more than once constrained to help them with money. On the occasion of my first visit after my removal, there were three or four of the brethren at work by candle light, after the close of their usual day's labour, removing the soil, to make ready for laying the floor; reminding me of the period of the Jews' return from their captivity, when it was said of them "the people had a mind to work." Nehemiah 4:6

The little chapel was completed within a shorter period than was at first anticipated, and I have more than once been permitted in my subsequent visits to unite with the dear saints in their worship, some of whom were previously unknown to me, having been converted after my departure.

> "Therefore my brethren, dearly beloved and
> longed for, my joy and crown, so stand fast in the
> Lord, my dearly beloved."—Philippians 4:1

CHAPTER XXX

MASTER AND SERVANT

"And he said, O Lord God of my master Abraham,
I pray thee send me good speed this day, and shew
kindness unto my master Abraham."—Genesis 24:12

A RIGHT understanding of the truth of God, obtained by prayerful reading of His word under the teaching of the Holy Ghost, will best enable us to fulfil the duties connected with the several relations of life. The parent and the child the husband and the wife, the master and the servant, may thus learn how to walk so as to please God, and to promote each others mutual happiness while passing through this evil world.

Some years ago I lived near one of the converted labourers on the farm mentioned in Chapter XXIV. His cottage was close to my own, and there was no other within a quarter of a mile. John M—— was a widower, and his three children were cared for by his mother-in-law, who was also a sincere Christian. His wages at this time were not more than eight shillings a week, but he was a man of a loving and liberal spirit, and delighted to serve others to the utmost of his power. On my coming to be his

> **SCRIPTURE TESTIMONY**
>
> *Love and honor one another
> in brotherly affection*
>
> ROMANS 12:10

neighbour, he told me there was a rick of wood in his garden which he wished me to use from, at any time without applying to him, and as I endeavoured to show him similar kindness, we lived in the utmost harmony, undisturbed by any untoward event during the eighteen months of my sojourn there. Among many instances of his generosity, one is especially worthy of record. On returning one day from the village, I mentioned the case of a poor woman there who was in great distress, and he immediately said he would send her a loaf when his children went to school the next morning. On my saying he need not do this as I had already helped her, he replied "But I shall though, for you know that for every penny we give in this way the Lord sends twopence." When he called on me *the next evening* he told me he had sent the loaf and few potatoes and a small piece of bacon. He soon after said "and what do you think the Lord has sent *me* to day? a seventh part of a fat sheep!" (I found this sheep had received some injury which induced his kind master to kill it, and divide it among his seven workmen.) He then 'said with a smile "now *didn't I tell* you the Lord would send twopence for the penny?" This incident beautifully illustrates the truth in Proverbs 11:24-25 "There is that scattereth and yet increaseth &c.;" and so also does another little circumstance which occurred nearly at the same time.

> SCRIPTURE TESTIMONY
>
> *Give and it shall be
> given unto you*
>
> LUKE 6:38

John was returning from the morning service on the Lord's day with three other men, when they met a poor Irish woman with her family, and her tale of distress induced three of the party to give her a trifle to help her on her way. Soon after, one of the party found a copper coin in the road, and presently other pence and halfpence were found, till all who had helped the poor woman had more than before, while he whose ear had been deaf to her tale of woe found nothing.

This dear brother's health began to decline about a year after I came to live near him, and through inflammation of the lungs he was for many months unable to labour. About the same time I went to visit a friend at some distance, who had recently much enlarged his house. Previous to my return home, he told me I could not do him a greater favour than by sending to his house any poor saint whose health needed change. He repeated the words, adding, "Remember I mean what I say, you can't do me a greater favour." I proposed to John to accept this kind offer, which he gladly did, and after some weeks he returned much benefited, though still unable to work. The friend whom he had visited cultivated a few acres of ground on the spade system, and kept four or five cows, and John remarked to me that the old man who laboured there was quite unfit for his work, adding that such a place would just suit him, as lie did not expect again to possess his former strength. He might perhaps have prayed about this, but he was too generous to wish to supplant another, or to covet his place. After a few months he renewed his visit, and was again treated with the greatest kindness and hospitality. After his return home when his health had further improved, he was one day surprised by the unexpected appearance of his friend, who having discerned his value during his two visits, had come to request his master to part with him. John left soon after to be his servant, and felt sure that the Lord had appointed him to this new scene of labour, for which he was especially qualified. Like the Eliezer of Abraham, he possessed the entire confidence of his new master. He bought and sold for him, and was allowed on any occasion when bethought it needful to employ another man to work under him. His duties were so well attended to that his master told me he did not know what he should do without John. I never remember to have seen a more Scriptural exhibition of a good master and a faithful servant than in John and his employer. The master sought to promote the servant's comfort and welfare, and the servant studied by every means to promote his master's interest, not with eye service as men pleasers, but as the servant of Christ doing the will of God from the heart. (Ephesians 6:6) He did not despise his master because he was a brother, (1 Timothy 6:2) nor did the master exact more than was due from the servant because he was ready to obey him. (Ephesians 6:9)

Of both characters Jesus is the perfect example. As the servant He delighted in the work the Father had given Him to do, and declared that this was His meat. (John 4:34) Obedience and submission marked His whole service while on earth, and when the last deep scene of agony began to open before Him, He still said, "If this cup may not pass from me except I drink it, thy will be done." Matthew 26:42. As the Master we see in all His conduct to His disciples gentleness, kindness, and love, while one of His last acts was to wash their feet to teach them to love each other as He had loved them.

It afterwards appeared that the value of a truly faithful servant was observed and appreciated by others. When I last saw him, about five years ago, he told me that a gentleman who wanted a confidential servant came to him and tried to induce him to leave his place, tempting him by the offer of twenty shillings a week; exactly double the wages he was at that time receiving. But he nobly resisted the temptation by replying that lie believed he was sent to his present place by the Lord, and he would riot quit it for the prospect of pecuniary reward. The wisdom and grace of this beloved brother was further manifested by the fact that up to the day I saw him he had not informed either his master or his wife (for he was again married at this time) of the offer he had received. Such truly disinterested conduct needs no comment, but it is sure to obtain that blessing of the Lord which "maketh rich and addeth no sorrow." Proverbs 10:22. He had already received an earnest of this by the conversion of his two daughters while quite young. Since the time alluded to I have not heard much respecting him, but both the master and his only child have lately been taken into rest.

It is instructive to observe that the desire of the rich brother to minister to the comfort of the Lord's afflicted people by receiving them into his house, was the means by which the Lord gave him the servant he so highly valued; and the kind liberality of the poor brother was amply rewarded by the Lord's sending him to a place so peculiarly fitted to his circumstances. He used no exertion to obtain this, but waited; on Him who hath said "Delight thyself also in the Lord, and he shall give thee the desire of thine heart." Psalm 37:4

Public attention has lately been called to the death of a rich man, whose history forms a painful contrast to that of this poor servant of Christ. By persevering industry and ceaseless toil he is said to have acquired an immense fortune, but no records are given of any acts of liberality or benevolence. Mammon seems to have been his god, and his object was to acquire gold. But it appears to have brought him no happiness, for he became deprived of the power to enjoy that which he had lived to obtain. In the midst of affluence it was his misery to believe himself a *poor man,* and the man of millions received wages for daily labour in his own park, to quiet his fear of dying in a work-house.

"The ground of a certain rich man brought forth plentifully, and he thought within himself, saying, what shall I do, because I have no room where to bestow my fruits? and he said this will I do; I will pull down my barns and build greater, and there will I bestow all my fruits and my goods; and I will say to my soul, soul thou hast much goods laid up for many years; take thine ease, eat, drink and be merry, But God said unto him, thou fool, this night thy soul shall be required of thee. Then whose shall those things be which thou hast provided? So is he that layeth up treasure for himself, and is not rich towards God." Luke 12:16-21

℘

While residing at Coleford it was my privilege to enjoy much happy communion in service with a beloved brother labouring in the gospel at Coleridge, and my "Recollec-

SCRIPTURE TESTIMONY
Communities of new believers formed by the Gospel
ACTS 2:42-47

tions" would be incomplete if I omitted a brief notice of the work there, on which the Lord has bestowed such large blessing. About thirty years ago I remember to have heard a letter read to me which was written by his sister, stating that she was the only believer in the parish, but expressing her confidence that the Lord had much people in that place. Some time after she had the happiness to witness the conversion of several of her relations, among whom was this dear brother, who up to this period had been thoroughly immersed in sporting, and other worldly amusements, but was now called to renounce the world and follow Christ. After a severe mental struggle, he was at length made willing, and began to preach the gospel. Of the blessing that has followed it will be sufficient to say that three chapels, each larger than the former, have been successively erected for the accommodation of the numerous hearers who assemble from different villages scattered around; and in this place where a few years since there was but one believer, there are now about one hundred and fifty who meet at the Lord's table in remembrance of His dying love, besides which very many others have either left the neighbourhood, or have fallen asleep in Christ. The work of conversion is still going on. On last Good Friday I beheld six hundred persons gathered together in this isolated locality, and could not help exclaiming "What hath God wrought!"

> "Brethren, pray for us that the word of the
> Lord may have free course, and be glorified,
> even as it is with you." 2 Thessalonians 3:1

CHAPTER XXXI

RETROSPECT

"Thou shalt guide me with thy counsel, and afterwards receive me to glory."—Psalm 73:24

IT has already been stated that towards the close of 1845 my mind became exercised about removal. The feeling was similar to that which I experienced at High Bickington seven years previous, arising from a consciousness that my work in and

SCRIPTURE TESTIMONY
Holy Spirit directs believers in ministry
MATTHEW 10:19-20 · ACTS 8:29 · ACTS 13:2 · ACTS 15:28 · ACTS 16:6-10 · ACTS 20:22 · ROMANS 8:14

near Coleford was completed, and that I was to remove elsewhere. Conversions had been very rare in the last two years, and my hope was that by going into some other locality, where the gospel was but little known, I might be used for further blessing. If I had been conscious of any motive of personal interest, as actuating me in my desire to change, it would have cost me much more anxiety, from a fear of acting contrary to the mind of the Lord, and of being tempted like Lot when he saw before him the well watered plains of Jordan. Genesis 13:11. This however was not my case. I have always felt the removal into a new locality, where the ministry is much, if not wholly, confined to the poorer classes, to be connected at first with much trial, arising from the fact of being thrown entirely among strangers, and also from an entire lack of social communion; in addition to this, the trouble and cost of removal are by no means desirable. I had on this occasion engaged to rent my cottage for three years, on account of the expense incurred by the landlord in making it convenient for me, and as only half that period was expired, I had the prospect of paying rent for two houses for some time to come; these things were all in favour of my remaining where I was, especially as I was truly happy in my intercourse with the Lord's dear people. But none of these things had the smallest effect in removing the impression, which I believe came from the Lord, that my work there was finished. I spoke of it as a certainty, though entirely ignorant as to where I might go, so that when a mason came to do some little work which he had for some time delayed, I told him he should have come before, as I was now going to leave the neighbourhood.

During the previous summer I had visited some friends in Somersetshire, near a village where there was a remarkable work of the Lord going on in conversion, and the thought had occurred to me that at some future time, I might be called into that locality. My visit was repeated in January 1846, and on this occasion a village was mentioned to me, the inhabitants of which were very numerous, and the gospel was much needed. This place was entirely unknown to me, but the mention of it excited in my mind the most determined resistance. I can only account for this by supposing it to be the result of powerful temptation. After two days, during which I was most anxious to know the Lord's will, a sudden reaction took place in my mind, and I was led to believe that the village, Merriott, was the spot intended for me. I first went to the place which was to be my residence for the next eight years, to enquire after a house, and my confidence seemed to gain strength, by finding a vacant cottage, just such as I needed, with a large malthouse attached, which might be rented and used for our meetings.

I had much cause for thanksgiving while retracing the events of the last seven years previous to my removal. The gospel during that period had been introduced into five different places, in four of which many souls had been converted, the whole number being not less than from eighty to one hundred; and four dear brethren remained to minister among them, all of whom had been raised up by the Lord during that period, and three of them remain there still. But for this, I should not have so plainly seen my way to remove.

The last conversion before my departure, was that of a poor man who wished to have ministry in his cottage, and as he was unknown to me, I called to see him a few days previous. He was at work in his garden, and after some other conversation I expressed my confident hope that as the Lord had given him the desire to receive the gospel into his *house,* He would also give him grace to receive it into his *heart.* Little did I then imagine how soon this was to be realised, but on my coming there to minister the next week, he walked home with me, to tell me how much these words had affected him, and I had no reason afterwards to doubt the reality of the Lord's work in his soul. I ministered only a few times at his cottage, as there was no encouragement, the number who came to hear being so small, but the Lord's purpose was answered in this dear mans conversion; and in thus using me to glean the last grape of my vintage at Coleford.

CHAPTER XXXII

A DEPRAVED VILLAGE

"The heart is deceitful above all things, and desperately wicked; who can know it"—Jeremiah 17:9

WITHIN three months from the time when I first felt assured I was to leave Coleford, I had removed to a village which I had not previously seen, nor had I spent six hours in the place until I came there to reside. Yet I had a confident persuasion that my steps were directed by the Lord. While on my way there, I was told, by one who well knew the place, that of fourteen hundred inhabitants, not more than one hundred attended any church or chapel. This was perhaps an extreme statement, though the general indifference to spiritual things was such as almost seemed to warrant it. I was not discouraged at this, but expressed my sure confidence that the Lord had many souls to call to Himself in that place, and in this I was not mistaken. The prospect however was at first very gloomy; like most other large villages where the light of the gospel has shone but feebly, the grossest immorality abounded, with almost heathen ignorance. Many of the inhabitants were known thieves, and imprisonment and subsequent transportation for offences of this character were not uncommon. One of the first conversions was that of a woman whose brother, and her husband's brother also, were transported. I had never witnessed such awful depravity, yet the people were generally kind to each other, and grateful for any kindness shown them. Lawlessness and independence were perhaps their prominent characteristics, which may have arisen from the circumstance that even the poorest cottager formerly lived in his own freehold, (as is still the case with many) but from inability to keep their dwellings in repair, they had in many eases suffered them to fall to the ground, or had sold them for a mere trifle in order to obtain parish relief. The population is so dense that of about three hundred houses it was a rare circumstance to see one of them unoccupied for a month. The poverty of the inhabitants is extreme, such as would scarcely be credited, and their ignorance equals their poverty. An aged man who was once a smuggler, and had both a son and grandson transported for theft, told me he had been to no place of worship since he was married. He lived in his own house, and I have often witnessed his simple meal of bread and water. Another person who sent for me when he was ill in bed, said he was *not a sinner,* evidently not knowing the meaning of the word, for previous to my leaving him he said he *would not cheat any more,* but in future give good weight and measure. He also said that except at his marriage, he had never been inside any church, chapel, or school in his life. This may possibly be a sample of many others, as it was far more common on the Lord's day to meet persons in their working dress than in any other. Indeed, there were many living near me who appeared not to possess any other. This may give some idea of the place where I was to reside eight years, and of the people among whom after a short acquaintance, I was, in spite of their depravity, pleased and content to dwell.

I first preached there on the Lord's day after my arrival, when the kitchen of my cottage was filled to overflowing, and for several succeeding weeks the whole of the ground floor, containing three rooms and a lobby, was densely crowded. At the end of two months, I rented the adjoining malt-house at four shillings a week, when the number of hearers so increased that we had for a long time a congregation varying from two hundred to four hundred persons. Each of the two first sermons in that place were used by the Lord for the conversion of an immortal soul.

Some time after my arrival I was informed of a circumstance relative to the first entrance of the gospel into the village some years previ-

SCRIPTURE TESTIMONY
Individuals opposed to the Gospel
ACTS 8:3 · ACTS 9:1-2

ous, which much interested me. The cottage I now occupied was at that time the property of a gentleman who lived in it, and who was much opposed to the truth. Three other individuals of respectability united with him in showing enmity to the gospel. My informant well remembered a summers evening, when on account of the heat, the preaching was held in the open air opposite to my gate, and the four persons were present annoying and ridiculing the preacher. One of them offered half-a-crown to any one who would procure a pitcher of water to throw over the small congregation, which was willingly done. Some time after the person who gave the money, when walking *near the very spot,* was observed to wander between the shafts of a waggon which lay there. He was suddenly seized with a paralytic stroke, which soon ended in death! The person living in my house afterwards died suddenly through the accidental discharge of his gun when about to step into his gig. Another of the party failed in business and went to America, where he became a confirmed drunkard, and the fourth died soon after I came to the village, after being for many years confined to his house a great sufferer by rheumatic gout. He has been heard to say that whenever he died he knew the devil would have him. Truly "the way of transgressors is hard." "Verily there is a God that judgeth in the earth."

I know not whether the report of my cottage being haunted arose from the sudden death of its former proprietor[11], but it is certain

---

11 Stories of his being seen on the premises were sometimes circulated while I was there, and some persons were afraid to go through the garden after dark. It may be partly owing to this that my garden crops were so respected, while the produce of others was frequently stolen just as it began to ripen. But their grateful appreciation of my endeavours to help them in their deep poverty might also

that it had not been permanently occupied for some years until it became my residence. Thus after being a long time vacant, it was tenanted by a minister of that gospel which its unhappy owner had so opposed and hated; and his malthouse also was destined to be used as the place in which it was the Lord's purpose to bring many precious souls out of darkness into His marvellous light.

---

have had this effect, as with very few exceptions the poor inhabitants, even the most depraved, were always ready to show me *any kindness* in their power.

CHAPTER XXXIII

THE CONVERTED BLIND BOY

"Wilt thou not from this time cry unto me, my father,
thou art the guide of my youth?"—Jeremiah 3:4

THE first conversion recorded in this volume was that of "blind George," and a dear boy who was blind, and whose name also was George, and whose conversion occurred subsequently to all the others, must be noticed in this chapter. His loss of sight was occasioned by his being struck by his schoolmaster with the hook of an umbrella. He was then about eleven years of age, and was soon after led by his mother to hear the gospel. Borne words about Jesus riding on the white horse, were fastened on his conscience, and awakened in his young mind deep conviction of sin. It was truly interesting to observe the gradual advancement of the Lord's work in his soul, and to hear his mothers account of his frequently stealing up stairs to pour out his heart to the Lord. She was herself the subject of similar experience, and I am not certain which of them were first blessed with a full sense of the Lord's pardoning love. The father, who was said to have been a Christian, had been dead some years, and this afflicted child, more dear from his blindness, was the especial favorite of the three children of the widowed mother. The sight of this dear boy at the Lord's table was exceedingly interesting during the few remaining months of his life, which was shortened by other disease resulting from the same accident. His end was peace, and his last words, uttered with a sweet smile, were "I go, I go." He had expressed much desire to be interred in the burying place near the chapel, and was much pleased when he was told his request would be granted, exclaiming "then I shall rise with the saints," perhaps supposing the ground was intended exclusively for the interment of the Lord's people.

A poor woman was converted about the same time, through being present while prayer was being offered for a person who was near death; and some particulars of her husband are too interesting to be omitted. His family was one of bad character, but unlike the other members of it, he was sober and industrious; but his temper was morose and peculiar. It was the constant practice of the wife to pray *for,* and *with* him, though often abused by him when on her knees, pleading with the Lord on his behalf; yet sometimes he was unable to refrain from weeping. Their first four children were girls, but they knew nothing of a father's love, or shared his smile. The two youngest being boys, were his *idols,* the only objects for which he seemed to have any affection. Like many agricultural labourers in over-populated localities, he often left home for a considerable time to procure work, and he had been long absent in one of the Channel islands, when he heard that all his children were dangerously ill with whooping cough. Had it been the *girls only,* he would probably have remained where he was, but the illness of the boys brought him home immediately. Deep was the anxiety with which he watched over them, as if his own life was bound up with theirs; and although he well knew his own state as a sinner, and that "the wages of sin is death," he said in his agony he could willingly have died in their stead. Those who have watched the dealings of the Lord in similar cases, will not be surprised to learn that the girls were spared, while the idols were taken away. I expressed to some my confident expectation that this affliction was sent for some purpose of blessing to their distressed father, who was at that time most willing to be prayed with, and to be reminded of the uncertainty of all earthly comforts and enjoyments. The two boys, who died nearly at the same time, were buried in one coffin. While preparing to leave my house on the following Lord's day, it *suddenly* occurred to my mind to preach on the prodigal son from Luke 15, and the subject on which I had intended to minister was set aside. I well remember to have enlarged on the condition of him who had "spent all" and "began to be in want," but without the slightest thought of the presence of the bereaved father, who had not been at our room for a long time. It appeared however that he also had been suddenly impressed with a desire to go to the room without any previous intention, (to use his own words, "all of a hop") and even without the knowledge of his wife. His heart was deeply affected by the discourse, and a great change was speedily visible in his whole conduct. He now came frequently to my house, and we had many affecting seasons in prayer together. Happy should I be to be able to say all I could desire about his future course; but although in his subsequent wanderings from home, he has sometimes fallen back, and his characteristic tempers have been afresh manifested, I have a confident hope that he has within him that "incorruptible seed which liveth and abideth for ever,"

It is not improbable that the heart of some affectionate parent may respond to this account of the father and his boys. Many like him have seen their error when too late; either by having to mourn the loss of those who were the objects of a fond partiality, or what is perhaps worse, to find their overweening affection repaid with ingratitude by their child while pursuing a course of sin and folly. Painful examples of this are not wanting, as every attentive observer must well know. The history of Eli may well excite reflection (see 1 Samuel 2) and awaken in Christian parents a desire to train up their children in the nurture and admonition of the Lord, while seeking to exhibit parental affection without partiality towards them all.

"Whatever passes as a cloud, between
The mental eye of faith, and things unseen;
Causing that brighter world to disappear,
Or seem less lovely, or its hopes less clear—
This is our *world*—our *idol*—though it wear
Affection's impress, or devotion's air."

CHAPTER XXXIV

DANGEROUS PROSPERITY

"Godliness with contentment is great
gain."— 1 Timothy 6:6

PERHAPS there is no temptation more common to the children of men, than the desire for riches, and in spite of the many examples of those who have proved their insufficiency to confer happiness, and the testimony of the word of God to the same truth, it is still the ruling-passion of mankind. To obtain wealth, men will brave any danger, endure any toil, and go to the furthest ends of the earth, each being destined in his turn, to prove that "all below the sun is vanity." "They that will be rich fall into temptation and a snare, and into many foolish and hurtful lusts," &c. 1 Timothy 6:9; and among the numberless instances in which this solemn truth has been realised, the following has lately come to my knowledge.

N. J—— was one of my earliest Sunday scholars at East Coombe, and was brought up to the trade of a carpenter. On his arrival at manhood, he went to reside in a village on the sea coast which was fast acquiring celebrity as a watering place, and being of an enterprising spirit he soon engaged in building speculations, in which he was generally successful. But the desire of wealth is not easily satisfied. The covetous man never says "I have enough," but like the daughters of the horse leech, he is still crying "Give, give." (Proverbs

151

30:15) To his own lawful occupation he added the dangerous one of an hotel-keeper, and not being satisfied with this, he commenced building another hotel, not far from that in which he lived. Through his marriage he subsequently became the owner of the largest hotel in the place, which had for many years been a flourishing concern. But he was not at ease. During the height of his prosperity he sometimes alluded to past scenes, and confessed that he had never been so happy as when pursuing his humble calling in his native village in quietness and peace. He remembered also the Sunday school, and spoke of his teacher with evident feeling, and still retained the little books which had formerly been given him. But these thoughts of past days soon gave place to the anxious cares of which he was continually the subject. It might have been truly said of him at this time "all his days are sorrow, and his travail grief, and his heart taketh not rest in the night, This also is vanity." Ecclesiastes 2:23. After awhile the tide of his prosperity began to ebb, and some reverses caused him to feel the pressure of deep solicitude. Happy would it have been, had he profited by this experience, and listened to His voice who invites the weary and heavy laden to come to Him, and find rest unto their souls. But there is no reason to hope that this was the case. He had not completed the building of the hotel, when after a short illness he "was removed out of time." His affairs were in great confusion, and as he had not calculated on an early death, he had made no arrangements concerning his property. When near his departure an attorney was sent for from a town at some distance, and a will was made which left the management of his affairs in the hands of a stranger, while the poor widow, through whom he became possessed of much of his property, derives but small benefit from it. It is hoped however that her deep trials have not been in vain, as having taught her to seek the imperishable riches which are made ours through faith in Christ Jesus. The two daughters are already blessed with the knowledge of His love.

The above particulars were related to me by one who was formerly his apprentice, and after his term of servitude commenced business on his own account. He was exposed to the danger of pursuing a similar course, by seeking to obtain some of the advantages which it offered to the enterprising and the industrious. But just at this time it pleased the Lord to reveal Christ to his soul, and the desire for earthly riches was checked by the knowledge of those precious blessings through which he was enabled to realise peace with God, and to receive the promise which declares "all things are yours—whether the world, or life, or death, or things present, or things to come, all are yours, and ye are Christ's, and Christ is God's." 1 Corinthians 3:21-23. The present purpose in this dear servant of God, is not to seek great things for himself, and he is daily proving that "a little which a righteous man hath is better than the riches of many wicked." Psalm 37:16

What sinners value I resign,
Lord 'tis enough that thou art mine;
I shall behold thy blessed face,
And stand complete in righteousness.

This life's a dream, an empty show;
But the bright world to which I go
Hath joys substantial and sincere;
When shall I wake, and find me there?

O glorious hour! O blest abode!
I shall be near, and like my God;
And flesh and sin no more shall be
A hindrance to my joy in thee.

My flesh may slumber in the ground;
But the last trumpet's joyful sound
Will wake the dust, and I shall rise
To meet my Saviour in the skies.

CHAPTER XXXV

SUDDEN DEATH

"If he set his heart upon man, if he gather to himself his
spirit and his breath; all flesh shall perish together, and
man shall return again unto death.'—Job 34:14-15

FEW subjects are more solemn, or more calculated to awaken
serious reflection, even in the most careless, than the sudden
removal of one "who is at ease in his possessions," and "counting
on long years of life to come." The church, the theatre, and the hall-
room have each been the scene of such events, and it was not long
since that a young man fell into the arms of death while threading
the mazes of the giddy dance. "This their way is their folly, yet their
posterity approve their sayings. Like sheep they are laid in the grave,
death shall feed on them; and their beauty shall consume in the grave
from their dwelling." Psalm 49:13-14. Yet strange as it may appear,
familiarity with the most solemn of all subjects generally weakens the
feeling of solemnity. The village grave digger, who has for many years
plied his trade in preparing the last habitation for scores or hundreds
of his neighbours, pursues his calling with as much indifference as if he
alone was immortal, and forgets that his successor will ere long provide
for him also the same narrow house. Yet oftentimes no one is more
witty, or more frequently at the alehouse than he who by his office is
so constantly reminded that "it is appointed unto men once to die."

These thoughts have in part been occasioned by a recent recollection of some instances of sudden death which have come under my immediate observation, which will form the subject of the present chapter.

More than fifty years ago, I went to the quay at Bristol to meet Captain R———, a gentleman with whom I was acquainted, who had just arrived in a coasting vessel from Devonshire. He was in advanced age, and remained in the ship while his niece, who accompanied him, went to procure lodgings. Little did either he or myself imagine that he was never to leave that vessel alive, yet so it was appointed by the Lord. While observing to me that his niece had been long away, he suddenly fell at my feet, and expired without a struggle or a groan. His niece soon returned, but only to order the lifeless body to be removed to the lodgings she had engaged.

Captain R——— was an officer in the navy, and his manners were most kind and courteous, but money was his idol; at the time of his death he had a belt containing gold coin round his person, but he was ignorant of the truth that "we are not redeemed with silver and gold, but with the precious blood of Christ," and that "riches profit not in the day of wrath."

A second instance is equally affecting. In the commencement of my ministry at East Coombe, I was one evening preaching with much enlargement, and while severally addressing the old, the young, and those in middle age, I well remember to have reminded the latter *that their sun might go down while it* was yet day (Jeremiah 15:9), and one at least of the hearers was speedily made to prove this. He was a mason, and in the full strength of manhood. He arose early the next morning to pursue his work, which he wished to finish in time to attend the revel. At this annual season, vice and folly reign triumphant. Men and women, youths and maidens, the grey headed sinner and the little child eagerly assemble, while the countenance of each too plainly declares that "there is no fear of God before their eyes." This poor man *intended* to go to the revel, in spite of the warning he had heard a few hours previously, but while at work on the roof of a farm house, he suddenly fell, and was immediately conveyed to his own cottage which was very near, It was yet morning when he was laid on the bed from which he was not again to rise. When I once saw him after the accident, he bitterly lamented his folly, but alas! it was *too late,* and there was no evidence of true repentance. "Oh that men were *wise,* that they *understood* this, that they would consider their latter end!" Deuteronomy 32:29. In a few days he was summoned into eternity.

The next solemn event occurred when I was on a visit to a friend at Coomb Martin, near the Bristol Channel. While walking out one morning, I observed a busy stir among the inhabitants, indicating that some event of general interest had taken place, and I was soon told the cause. Two poor men had just been buried beneath a mass of fallen earth, and I immediately followed those who were hastening to the fatal spot. This was close to a deep pit, connected with some mining operations, and it was at first supposed they might have fallen into it, but all doubts were soon ended by the removal of the earth which covered the dead bodies. Being little accustomed to such scenes, the sight of two fellow creatures who had lately been in full health, but within less than an hour had been hurried into eternity, (and if ignorant of Christ and His salvation into eternal misery) deeply affected me. Indeed all seemed to feel that death was present. Few words were spoken, and those in a very low tone of voice. Nearly all gazed in silence on the melancholy sight.

When the first body was extricated, and life was pronounced by a surgeon who was present to be extinct, a man who stood near me, said just loud enough for me to hear him "Poor fellow! I've often heard him say 'Twill never fall! *'Twill never fall!"* I concluded from this that the fall of this mass of earth had by some been anticipated, and that he who now lay dead before me had been warned of the danger, and had despised the warning till destruction fell on him.

While on my return, I passed the cottage of one of these poor men, and heard the wailing of his widow, as of one who refused to be comforted, exclaiming she had "lost her only friend," Yet I was afterwards informed that a few days before she and her husband had quarrelled even to blows!

Perhaps some reader of this solemn incident may be led to see in this poor man's indifference to friendly warning, a picture of their own state. For it is the state of all who make light of the gospel, rejecting its offers of mercy, and despising its warnings of judgment. The word of God declares that "all have sinned," and that "the wages of sin is *death.*" Romans 3:23, and 6:23. It also declares that the blood of Jesus Christ cleanses from all sin, 1 John 1:7, and offers a free pardon with eternal salvation to all who come to God through Him. But it also speaks of a time of judgment, which will ere long overtake and suprise a careless world. "For when they say, peace and safety, then sudden destruction cometh upon them, as travail upon a woman with child, and they shall not escape." 1 Thessalonians 5:3. The accident by which these two men so suddenly lost their lives affords but a feeble type of the ruin of all who reject the gospel of the Son of God, who compares Himself to a stone, and declares that "on whomsoever it shall fall it will grind him to powder." Matthew 21:44.

The above account of the miners had been written but a few days, when in June last I had occasion to leave home for a short time, and on my way to the railway station, I was seated in the omnibus opposite to one who was apparently drawing near the grave. Her appearance seemed to indicate that some time had been occupied that morning in decorating her fragile form, and a handkerchief in her hand contained some other articles, probably intended for further adornment on her arrival at the end of her journey. She said she was one of thirteen sisters, seven of whom had already died in consumption, and it was evident from her conversation that she was the subject of alternate hopes and fears respecting her own state. At one time she said "tell me I am not better, and I have *walked a mile* this morning!" and soon after "if I am not better in a month I shall give myself up," She was on her way to Cheltenham, and after a short visit there, was going, *as she hoped,* into Wales, and if this did her no good, she thought nothing more could be done for her. On being asked if she was happy, she replied with energy *"No*—I am *not!"* and soon after said "I have a great deal to do." She was reminded that all that was needful for our salvation was already accomplished, for the Son of God had shed His blood for all who believe on Him, and that faith in Him was the only way of salvation. But whether from the languor connected with the disease, or from indifference to the truth, she paid but little attention. I lost sight of her at the station, but was afterwards informed that before the conclusion of *that same* day, she was numbered with the dead!

Surely there is a voice in such a solemn providence to every unprepared soul that may read of it, "Go to now, ye that say to day or to morrow we will go into such a city—whereas ye know not what shall be on the morrow. For what is your life? it is ever a vapour, which appeareth for a little time, and then vanisheth away." James 4:13-14. Within a few hours after the above conversation, the gay apparel was exchanged for a winding sheet, and the wearer of it who had confessed that she had "a great deal to do," had passed into that eternal state of which it is said "there is no work nor device in the grave, whither thou goest." Ecclesiastes 9:10

The first of the following verses will express the thoughts of many.

> *"I will*—*to morrow*—*that* I will,
>   I will be *sure* to do it;
> To morrow *comes*—to morrow *goes,*
>   And yet *I am* to do it.
>
> And thus repentance is deferred
>   From one day to another,
> Until the day of death doth come—
>   And judgment is the other."

CHAPTER XXXVI

CONCLUSION

"Blessed be the Lord God, the God of Israel, who only
doeth wondrous things. And blessed be His glorious
name for ever, and let the whole earth be filled with
Hie glory. Amen and Amen"—Psalm 72:18-19

THE preceding chapters contain a brief detail of village labour
in the gospel from 1815 to 1847, beyond which period it is
not at present necessary to extend it. Some of the incidents
are written from memory and others from memorandums made at
the time they occurred; but I am not aware that there has been any
incorrectness even in the most trivial details, and the more prominent facts are related with strict truthfulness.

My object in publishing this memorial of past service will only be
partially accomplished if it merely tends to interest or amuse those
who may read it, or even if it should only excite some increasing
desire to further the work of the Lord. It is my hope that the Lord's
dear people maybe led to weigh well the facts here set before them, in
reference to the manner in which He has sustained a very unworthy
instrument in that work for twenty-five years, (the time commencing with Chapter XII) and also the measure of blessing with which
He has been pleased to accompany his simple and unpretending
statement of gospel truth.

The Christian reader is requested to notice the following facts in reference to that period.

1st.   During these twenty-five years my service for the Lord has been entirely among the poorest classes, and in places where there had previously been a very small measure of gospel light.

2nd. Within that time six companies of saints have been gathered into communion, and still continue to meet in the name of the Lord Jesus. A very large proportion of these were persons newly converted, and besides these there are three other companies in places where it was my privilege first to labour and prepare the way.

[Since this paragraph was written I have received tidings of the prosperity of the Lord's work, and of fresh conversions in four of these places.]

3rd.   All these places have from the commencement been supplied with ministry raised up by the Lord in their respective neighbour-hoods. Of the ten brethren who have been called into ministry, seven are the fruit of the gospel, the other three having been converted before.

4th.   During these twenty-five years no public collection has been made in any of these places for any purpose whatever. All contri-butions for poor saints, and for necessary expenses connected with our worship, being given on the first day of the week, (1 Corinthians 16:2) nor has help been at any time solicited, save from the Lord's people.

5th.   As my labours have been entirely among those who were unable to care for my temporal need, I have been cast on the Lord for nearly my whole support, for which He in His rich grace has abundantly provided; any occasional pressure causing trial of faith, having only tended to make the deliverance more sweet and precious, when in due time it arrived.

6th.   During these twenty-five years I have not purchased any article of the smallest value for which I had not the money to pay.

7th. Neither for myself, nor for any brother helping in the work, nor for the erection of any of the chapels, has application been made for help to any religious society.

8th. The conversions which the Lord has graciously granted, as the fruit of the gospel in the six places I have alluded to (besides those which were granted in the first thirteen years at Tawstock) cannot be less than from two to three hundred, and if to those are added the souls converted in my first place of service the whole number may be reckoned as not less than from three to four hundred and the ministry for these has cost nothing.

Surely it is not needful to say more to prove that simple and devoted labour for Christ, if entered upon in dependence on Himself alone, and persevered in with a single eye to His glory, will be crowned with abundant success. It will not indeed be recognised by men (who will praise thee if thou doest well to *thyself*) but the path of self denial, if it be one of reproach, will also be that of true blessing, for it is that which the Master has trod before us. He has sanctioned it by His example, and He still says to us in His word, "If any man *serve me*, let him *follow me*, and where I am there shall also my servant be. If any man serve me him shall my Father honour," John 12:20

There are still many dark places in our land where the gospel is needed, and where its glad tidings would be joyfully received. But the labourers are few. Should any faithful servant of Christ feel led by the statements contained in this volume, to give himself to such a work by seeking to make known "the unsearchable riches of Christ," in places where He is not yet known, this brief detail of village, labour will not have been issued in vain.

APPENDIX

APPENDIX

"Thou shalt remember all the way which the
Lord thy God led thee these forty years in the
wilderness," &c.—Deuteronomy 8:2

1832, MAY 5. — I informed my dear wife our funds were almost
exhausted, having but five shillings more than enough to pay for
a pair of shoes which were making for one of our children. A *few
minutes* after Mr. P—— told me he had orders to measure all my
children, and the pair he was then making would of course be
included.

May 10. — W. J—— a farm servant lately converted, sent me
eight bottles of cider which he had saved from his usual allowance.
When about to send it, it occurred to him that he was only giving
that which cost him nothing, when he added two pounds of butter
which he bought for the purpose.

June 11. — I had engaged
to accompany a dear brother,
R. C—— to day on a short
tour into some of the neighbouring villages, without
purse or scrip, and it was

SCRIPTURE TESTIMONY
God will provide for *our daily needs*
MATTHEW 6:11

ordered by the Lord that I should not only do this, but also leave my dear wife and children to be cared for by Him during my absence. We had but eightpence in hand the previous evening, and *this exact* sum was required for the carriage of a parcel before I left home; yet I never saw my dear wife more truly happy or feeling less anxiety than when about to be thus left for some days by her nearest earthly friend, with no help save that which arose from a lively faith in the promise of a covenant God.

June 17. — The Lord has not been unmindful of my dear wife in my absence, having sent Her money by two different hands, and also a basket of provisions.

SCRIPTURE TESTIMONY
Generously give to those in need
ACTS 4:32-37 · GALATIANS 6:2 · HEBREWS 13:16 · 1 JOHN 3:17

June 23. — This morning we had scarcely sufficient bread for our breakfast. Soon after a beggar came to our door asking for bread. It was the first time I had ever been without bread in my house, but I gave him the only halfpenny I had, and one farthing remained. *Very soon* after, the postman brought us a letter containing five pounds, the Lord thus graciously sending this large help in a time of great need. It is worthy of remark that this was the first occasion in which I had received any money by post since my return to Barnstaple.

Aug. 25. — I was enabled last week to send some tea, sugar, and coffee to a brother who had been unexpectedly deprived of many comforts, and on the *following Saturday* I received a parcel from a long distance, containing two pounds of tea, one of coffee, seven of sugar &c., the Lord returning to me almost immediately a larger supply of the same articles. (Proverbs 11:24)

A loaf was also sent to me this week by W. K—— (the Backslider in Chapter VIII) who is generally very poor, but "the liberal deviseth liberal things." Isaiah 32:8. His wife has been gleaning, and of the produce of her industry he sends to me and another brother also, a large loaf.

Nov. 2. — Two poor brethren of Tawstock sent me each a bag of potatoes, the fruit of their yearly harvest, and one of them was accompanied with a piece of pork.

Nov. 10. — My dear wife was going to market with only one shilling, but as she was leaving a dear friend called and walked with her; at parting she gave her a sovereign, the Lord inclining her heart thus to supply our need. How sweet to observe His hand in such events as these!

W. M— called to say he was ordered to measure me for a pair of boots. I had for some time anticipated the coming winter, but did not feel our means warranted my buying these, which however I much needed. This was only known to the Lord, who so graciously supplied them according to His promise. (Philippians 4:19) Oh for faith to trust in Him at all times!

My dear wife told me this morning she must buy a pint of brandy, which I knew she required and made no objection. But when she expressed a wish to purchase a bottle of wine also for my use, I objected, as there was not the same necessity and our means were small; yet I was at this time much wearied with over exertion in the Lord's work. On going soon after into our kitchen, *I saw a pint of brandy on the table,* which *had been brought there while we were talking about it,* with a canister of arrow root. The *next morning,* M. C—— told me a *bottle* of *wine* had been left for me at her house, and a day or two after Brother C—— told me he had a bottle of rum for me. While he was yet in the house, my aunt called and gave a sovereign to my dear wife, observing that I appeared weak, and begged her to buy me some *wine.* All this occurred within a few days, and how blessedly do these various circumstances prove the tender care of a loving Father towards His unworthy child. No one was made acquainted with our circumstances save Himself, who so sympathises with us in all our trials. It is to be observed that the *brandy* was sent *immediately,* as it was about to be purchased at once, and the cost of it would have diminished our small stock of money.

Nov. 15. — Our faith was much tried this morning, having no coals, and but little bread for breakfast. We sent for three bushels of coal, being the first occasion of our purchasing anything on credit. My dear Mary was in bed the early part of the day, which passed without our receiving any help.

SCRIPTURE TESTIMONY
Don't be anxious, for
He cares for us
MATTHEW 6:25-34 ·
1 PETER 5:6-7

Nov. 16 — Previous to rising this morning, Satan was permitted to harrass me with unbelieving fears, so that I was almost ready to say "this evil is of the Lord," &c. My dear Mary was unable to rise on account of weakness, and I was tried by not being able to get for her breakfast the things she needed, having no butter and but little bread. But our most gracious Lord was pleased to make our scanty meal one of the happiest I ever partook of, so that I could indeed say "My cup runneth over." While at breakfast the dear children repeated their texts for the day, all of which were so suitable and so unexpected also, that they were quite a feast to my soul. Those of the four eldest were as follows, "I will never leave thee, nor forsake thee." Hebrews 13:5. "Bread shall be given him; his water shall' be sure." Isaiah 33:16. "He hath given meat to them that fear Him, He will ever be mindful of His covenant." Psalm 111:5. "Seek ye not what ye shall eat, or what ye shall drink, neither be ye of doubtful mind." Luke 12:29

I do net remember ever to have enjoyed a more happy meal with my dear family, proving as it did theft "man liveth not by bread alone but by every word that proceedeth out of the mouth of the Lord," Deuteronomy 8:3, and it was a singular coincidence that both our reading and our hymn for that morning (which were in regular course) were so peculiarly suited to the occasion; the former being Romans 8, from verse 26 to the end, and the latter being three verses from the Cottage Hymn Book, the last being

"Only when the way is rough,
    And the coward flesh would start,

> Let thy promise and thy love.
> Cheer and animate my heart."

After breakfast we knew not whence our next meal was to come, and I was tempted to suggest to my dear wife our borrowing of some friend; but although so weak and needing many things, she stedfastly opposed this, desiring to look *only to the Lord*. And truly He proved Himself to be all sufficient, by sending that same day three shillings, and ten more the next morning, thus allowing me to pay for the coals purchased three days ago.

Oct. 21. — Went to preach to a congregation seven miles distant, which being destitute of ministry I visited once a fortnight at the request of a brother whose time was too much occupied to continue his service there. On my arrival I was told there was to be a collection, and another minister was coming to preach in my place, to add to my disappointment I had paid my last sixpence to the ferryman to take me across the river. But I felt it was well to be brought into some degree of conformity to Him who was a man of sorrows. My service in this place was entirely gratuitous, but I felt myself in this instance under bondage.

Oct. 23. — Having no bread I sent early for a loaf, saying *I would pay for it that morning,* and the Lord did not disappoint my expectation that He would enable me to do so. On calling to enquire for a sister in Christ, I was told she wished to see me, which she had not been well enough to do for some time past. At parting she gave me a sovereign, which I received just in time to pay for the loaf *in the morning* as I had promised, and to provide other things for dinner,

(This loaf, and the coals a week previous, are the only articles we purchased on credit. I was then but young in the way, and my peculiar trials were severe, but the Lord was tender to my infirmities. I do not wish on this account to justify my failure which I have here recorded, but rather to be humbled for it. I have since found the comfort of waiting on the Lord, until in *His own* time, He was pleased to send deliverance.)

Dec. 1. — Five pounds were sent me as a legacy of love from O. P—— the dear sister I saw for the last time so lately. Another proof this of our Lord's tender care, especially as the health of my dear wife is such as to render many little comforts necessary.

Dec. 13. — Two sovereigns were given to my dear wife in aid of the expense connected with her removal to High Bickington, where she wishes to go for change. *We had just before been conversing about this expense.*

Jan. 11. — On Wednesday I was led to pray for the money for a mattrass we had ordered at a time when we had the cost of it in our hand, but being delayed longer than we expected, it was now spent. *Before I left my room,* I was called on by a friend who said on leaving "I shall give you half a sovereign when I next see you," this is, I believe, exactly the sum required.

(I have since seen that in all similar cases the cost of any article so ordered, should he laid by as for a thing already purchased.)

My dear wife's lodgings have greatly increased our expenses, but this has been met by the kind offer of a dear friend to defray the whole cost of them while she remains at High Bickington.

(The above extracts relate to the few months of our residence at Barnstaple. They were the first days of our new path of dependence, and our trials were not few. Our need was sometimes greater than at any subsequent period., and to me the trial was much increased by the declining health of my dear wife, who was evidently fast hastening to the grave. Yet in our deepest sorrow we neither of us had a thought of returning to our former position, being fully assured that we were in the path which the Lord had marked out for us, and the consciousness of this gave us strength to hear with cheerfulness His holy will. I was led especially to see at this time that the Lord will *prove* any measure of faith which we may *profess to have received from Him,* and that His method of doing this may sometimes be as by fire. (I Peter 1:7)

1833, Jan. 19. — Owing to some unpleasant neighbours who came to live next door to us, I saw clearly the Lord's mind to quit the house. We left it therefore this day, and I joined my dear wife at High Bickington, which is to be our future residence.

Feb. 11. — The health of my dear wife affords ground for serious apprehensions as to the result. But *Jesus* is a *rock,* and His way is perfect. He will not suffer His people to be moved. Of our afflictions, as of our mercies, it may be said they seldom come alone, and sometimes, as at the birth of Gad we are ready to say "a troop cometh."

Feb. 23. — In addition to my other sorrows, I have to lament the departure of my beloved and very aged mother. On returning this day from Topsham, where she was interred, I found one of the brothers and a sister of my dear wife with her. They were much affected by her appearance, and wish to remove her to her father's house for the benefit of change and nursing.

Feb. 26. — My dear wife was taken this day to Natson, and my forebodings are that she will not return again to this place. Her last act was to seek a lodging for me at a small farm near the village, which though very humble, is convenient enough for one who professes to be a stranger and a pilgrim on the earth.

March 29. — The remains of my beloved wife were interred this day at East Coombe; a solemn season to all, but we sorrow not as others who have no hope.

SCRIPTURE TESTIMONY
God provides exactly what is needed
2 CORINTHIANS 8:15 · PHILIPPIANS 4:19

April 1. — One circumstance connected with my late trial must not be unnoticed. The funeral expenses were to one in my circumstances considerable, but I was not allowed to be anxious about this, and the Lord's gracious interposition on my behalf was very remarkable. Within a few hours after my dear wife's departure, I was told that a sum of money had just been received from a distance for the help of those who were labouring in the gospel, by some individuals to whom I was not personally known, and of this sum I was requested to accept thirteen pounds, being amply sufficient to defray all my expenses.

(I consider this to be one of the most remarkable instances I had hitherto experienced of the Lord's gracious care. Indeed *who ever* trusted in Him and was confounded? I am not aware that I had one anxious thought in the expectation of this need, nor could I have supposed that it would have been supplied through such a channel. I have never heard who the parties were whom the Lord used as His instruments in furnishing this supply, nor the quarter from whence it came.[12])

June. — The poverty of some of my neighbours being severe, I wrote to a benevolent brother for money to help them, and took the letter to Barnstaple to post it. On entering the town I met a friend who desired me to call on Miss ——, who had something for me from the very individual to whom my letter was addressed, and of course I did not post it. I now found that ten pounds had been sent by him, two of which were for the poor, and the remainder for my own use. How wonderful are the ways of our God, and how abundant is His mercy and lovingkindness towards those who trust in Him!

March 20. — J. B——, a dear brother in Christ, came to see me previous to his departure for America, where he intended to labour in the gospel. My circumstances at this time were very low; he told me the Lord has sent him such abundant supplies that I must share a part with him. Finding I was not willing to speak of my circumstances, he constrained me to accept a five pound note. After our prayer meeting, he called me aside and said that on turning over his notes he had past one of ten pounds, which he felt he ought to have given me instead of the five, and he should not be happy in his conscience unless I allowed him to exchange it, and thus correct his mistake. The grace and tenderness of conscience exhibited by this dear brother will be appreciated by all who "know the grace of our Lord Jesus Christ."

April 6. — Having for some time needed a great coat, and being on a journey to Exeter, I called on a brother who was a tailor, who told me where he thought I could be well served. The following

---

12   From this period the extracts are not in consecutive order, and the date of the year is omitted.

evening, when on my way to a meeting for reading the scriptures, I passed the shop to which I had been directed, and the circumstance was brought to my remembrance, but thinking it might be prudent to defer it for the present, I passed on. After the meeting, the brother at whose house it was held, put a paper into my hand containing a sovereign and a half, which I immediately thought was sent me by the Lord for the great coat, as the amount added to a smaller sum which had been given me since I left home, was just the sum required, and it was purchased the next morning.

March 1. — My temporal supplies were short, and I felt entirely cast on the Lord for means to enable me to remove to Bow. I observed to Brother P—— this morning, that although the day of my departure was fixed I had not as yet money enough to pay for the carriage of my furniture. It was but a *few minutes* after this, when classing the road to my own house, a letter was put into my hand containing five pounds from the saints at P——. It was the first time they had thus sent to me, and the supply came as from the Lord for this especial time. Four sovereigns were also sent me from other quarters previous to my leaving.

May 18. — Our faith was much tried, having little provisions and scarcely coal enough to last through the day; added to this we expected a friend from High Bickington to spend a week with us. But the Lord who *knew* our need had also *provided* for it. Our young friend, who came at the expected time, informed us that she had travelled part of the way with W. H——, a dear brother in Christ, who on finding she was coming to see us, sent by her hand thirteen shillings. One shilling was also sent by a poor brother at High Bickington. Jehovah Jireh!

(It will be observed that I have frequently mentioned the gifts of poor believers, and to these I might add hundreds more. But I have not endeavoured so much to show the *amount* of the things sent me, as the *love* by which these poor saints were led to furnish their various offerings; their "deep poverty abounding to the riches of their liberality." I have sometimes received a single sixpence sent by a poor brother living some scores of miles from me, and such an offering is very precious in His sight, "who though He was rich, yet for our sakes He became poor.")

> ### SCRIPTURE TESTIMONY
>
> *God will provide for our daily needs*
>
> MATTHEW 6:11

June 10. — I was invited to attend a meeting at L—— to consider some questions connected with prophecy, my travelling expenses being kindly offered me. At the close of the meeting, on the evening previous to my leaving, it occurred to me whether I had sufficient money to pay my way home, as I wished to extend my journey into Hertfordshire to see my dear children who were there at school. On returning to my lodgings I was led to pray much about this, and just at midnight the Lord graciously composed my mind by bringing to my remembrance the words "This is my infirmity, but I will remember the years of the right hand of the Most High." Psalm 77:10. In a moment the temptation was gone and the matter was left in the Lord's hand. I had appointed to meet several brethren at six the next morning, and proceed with them in a carriage to the nearest station, but on my arrival I found there was no room, the carriage being already full. Another brother arrived soon after, and was also disappointed, but he kindly bade me not to be anxious as we would go together. He then hired a phaeton, and waited to the latest moment to take a third party, whom we were obliged to leave behind. We had thus to travel eight or ten miles alone, and it is sweet to observe the Lord's hand in such events as these. I did not make the slightest allusion to my own circumstances, but just as we were getting near the station, my companion asked me *if I thought I had money enough to pay my way home;* and on my replying I did not know, he put into my hands five sovereigns. It was now seen why I was disappointed of my place in the first carriage, and why I was to travel alone with the kind brother who so liberally helped me on my way. In this gracious way did the Lord show me that my anxiety on the previous night was my infirmity, and that His resources were sufficient for all my need.

May 15. — J. H——, a poor brother, came to my door with a donkey, and said, "The Lord has sent you something." This was about two hundred weight of potatoes, which we much needed at this time. On my enquiring if any one had desired him to bring them, he said "No! the Lord told me that you wanted them, and that I must bring them to you."

About the same time the postman passing through the village after we were in bed, blew his horn outside our door. When I came down and opened it I found he had left a basket containing a leg of mutton and other provisions.

Nov. 22. — This day the carrier brought me a basket containing thirteen bottles of wine, which at first I refused to receive, as it was not directed, nor was any letter sent with it; but I was assured it was for me, though the carrier did not know the name of the party that sent it. It was at this time very acceptable and much needed. For a long time I had no clue to discover from whence it came, but at last found it was the gift of a clergyman, a distant relative (though nearly related in Christ), whom I had not seen for fifteen years.

July 11. — We were visited to-day by two sisters in the Lord. After they had left we found a note directed to me containing five pounds, with the words, "A small debt, according to 2 Corinthians 9:7-14;" and also a small parcel containing a sovereign, with the words, "From a sister in the Lord—a sister —a fellow-servant."

Sept. 22 — On returning home this evening I found a letter on the table containing five pounds, with the words, "Beloved, I wish above all things that thou mayest prosper and be in health even as thy soul prospereth." In this bountiful manner is the Lord supplying my need; but that which is vastly more gratifying is the manifest blessing on His own word, gladdening my heart by causing me to witness the conversion of many souls to Himself, and also delivering many dear saints from fear and bondage.

Nov. 30. — A sister in the Lord sent me ten pounds to purchase a pony, which my wide scene of labour rendered necessary. Finding that the one first purchased did not suit me, five pounds more were sent by another servant of Christ to enable me to exchange it. Both these gifts were quite unexpected by me.

Sept. 1. — G. A——, a poor brother from Woodland Head came to see me, bringing a small loaf and some cream, he having heard me admire their household bread when I once took tea at his cottage. This kind offering was brought a distance of four miles. The wages of this dear brother are but seven shillings a week, yet on the same morning he gave sixpence to one of his sick brethren at Coleford. How precious are these tokens of love in the sight of Him who laid down His life for our sakes!

Oct. 24 — I had purposed this morning to go to a meeting of brethren many miles distant, and to remain from home about a week, but my means were too limited to allow me to leave any money at home for the support of my family. I had never done this on any previous occasion, but my dear children were so anxious that I should not forego this privilege, that they earnestly requested me to undertake the journey, and expressed their full confidence that the Lord would care for them during my absence. It was my purpose to comply with their wishes though it would involve some measure of trial to leave them thus; but the Lord in His great mercy did not allow me to be thus tried. A few hours previous to my leaving, a letter was received enclosing ten pounds. O for grace to trust in Him at all times!

May. 22. — I received this day an anonymous paper with the following words : "I am directed to send to Mr. R. G—— the sum of ten pounds. Please to acknowledge the receipt of the same to Mr. —— of ——

"'It is *more* blessed to give than to receive.'"

It was some time ere I knew by whom this timely help was sent, but subsequently found that it came from one of the Lord's servants, to whom I was an entire stranger, and whose name I had never before heard. Surely it is not a vain thing to trust in the Lord.

Jan. 15. — I was led while in prayer this morning to ask the Lord to send me money this very day," an expression I never remember to have used before, and on going to the post office I received a letter enclosing an order for three pounds.

Dec. 10. — My mind had for some time been exercised about leaving this neighbourhood, believing that the Lord had work for me elsewhere, and I told my daughter a short time ago I was now *sure* we should soon quit it, yet without the slightest idea respecting our future dwelling place. I added also that if my impression was correct, and in accordance with the Lord's mind, he would send me twenty pounds to meet the expense of change of residence, feeling sure that my future place of service would be at a greater distance than that of any previous removal. A *few days* after this conversation (at which a third person was present) I received from a very unexpected quarter a cheque for ten pounds. This seemed to confirm my thought of leaving, especially as it came from one who had never sent to me in this way before. Other supplies followed so abundantly that within one month I received from various quarters twenty-eight pounds three shillings and sixpence. (It may be remembered that on a former occasion when I was about to remove twenty miles, five pounds were unexpectedly sent me; now the distance to which I was to be sent was sixty miles, and the larger sum being needed was graciously supplied.

Aug. 17. — I received this day five shillings, sent me by W. H—— a poor brother in Devonshire, being the first help sent me from that county where I laboured in the gospel for thirty years, since I quitted it five months ago, and it came from one who earns his daily bread by the sweat of his brow. This is truly "a savour of a sweet smell, acceptable to God through Jesus Christ."

(This dear brother on a former occasion sent me a sack of potatoes. Previous to his conversion he had been discharged by his former master for dishonesty. What a change does the grace of God make in the heart of a poor sinner! He who used to *steal* can now *give*, and for a poor man, liberally, to one whom he regards as his father in the gospel. On my speaking to this dear man after preaching next door to his cottage he was *offended*, but on the next occasion of my coming there, the *Lord* spake to him by the word of His truth, and he was *converted.)*

Sept. 28. — We received into our family Mary Marks, a poor and very afflicted young person lately converted. Her parents are both dead, and her heart complaint does not allow her to take any active exertion. We have confidence that the Lord will accept our poor service on behalf of this His afflicted child as being done to Himself.

Sept. 28. — This morning we had only three shillings in hand, and we were expecting a servant of the Lord to spend several days with us. Soon afterwards a sovereign was found in the box at the room directed to me, and another was sent us the day our friend arrived. Our need was known to our Heavenly Father and Oh! how watchful is His care who causes that need to furnish fresh occasions for the exhibition of His faithfulness and love!

July 11. — My frequent attacks of nervous despondency caused me to desire a donkey and chaise, in which to ride out occasionally, and I began to lay by some money for this purpose. But my supplies soon grew short, and I was led to doubt whether it was according to the Lord's mind to lay by money for this purpose, and when my other means became exhausted, I determined to use what I had laid up and leave the matter in the Lord's hands. The result is worthy of being pondered and remembered. *Only a few minutes* after I had come to this resolution I received a letter informing me that a brother in the Lord who had heard of my need had a donkey and chaise in view, and hoped soon to send them to me as a token of his Christian love. It is sweet to observe how gently and tenderly the Lord corrects the mistakes of His children, "He remembers that we are dust." (The donkey and chaise were soon afterwards sent, but the poor animal so tried my patience that I could not long use him. The Lard however helped me soon after to procure a pony which fully answered my purpose.)

Sept. 21. — For some time my supplies have been more than usually limited, perhaps to lead me into a more habitual dependence on the Lord, who in His rich grace generally sends deliverance when the moment of trial comes on. On rising this morning my whole stock of money, amounted to *five-pence,* but within an hour after the post brought me a letter containing *five pounds,* which the writer states to have been sent him by a friend for my use, adding that he wished to write me more fully but he felt *pressed to send it by that day's post.* I have seldom discerned the Lord's hand more distinctly than on this occasion. O that it may teach me more to confide in His love and to "trust in Him at all times."

Feb. 23. — This morning I gave my Polyglot Bible to one of my daughters the type being too small for me. Half an hour after this Brother C——,who had passed the night at our house, remarked that he had lately purchased a Polyglot Bible of a larger type than he had previously seen. After the morning service my daughter was desired by Mrs. R—— to walk a little way with her, and while doing so she observed a larger book than usual in her basket, and was told it was a Polyglot Bible which had lately been sent to her by her son. On my daughter's observing it was just what I wanted she offered her to take it home for me to see, and desired her to return it in the afternoon. On her way home she was overtaken by a brother who was coming to see me, and on their arrival the bible was shown to me and the brother just come wished to see it. While at dinner he remarked that on his way to my house he had been asking the Lord how he could show me some token of his love, winch he now desired to do by procuring for me a copy of this bible. All I have related took place in less than five hours, and all the links in this chain of circumstances tend to exhibit the providential arrangements of our Father in Heaven who careth for us.

Sept. 16. — Being about to commence packing my furniture previous to removal, and feeling weak, I wrote a note to send for a bottle of wine, but *before the note left my house* a friend brought me two bottles of excellent wine, being the gift of a brother in the Lord living more than thirty miles off, whom I had not seen for some years.

May 1. — I received this day by post an order for two pounds. On the envelope was written "with F. H——'s Christian regards." The post mark was St. John's Wood, but I have no recollection of any one bearing the name of which I have given the initials. If this should meet the eye of the kind donor she will please accept my thankful acknowledgments.

March 24. — This was a day of trial, but our minds were kept in peace. We looked to the Lord for help and expected it, but as the post brought us no letters all expectation for this day was given up. But just at its close the deliverance came, a letter being brought by a messenger inclosing five pounds, filling our hearts with thanksgiving and praise.

Dec. 23. — I received this day a 'basket containing a duck, a hare, and some cream from one of the dear saints at High Bickington. A sweet token of their love after many years absence and being nearly eighty miles distant from each other.

April 24. — My funds were reduced to three shillings, when on leaving B—— yesterday a sovereign was put into my hand, and on arriving home two letters were waiting for me, one containing three, and the other ten pounds.

July 18. — We could not have got on after this day without help, but my mind was kept free from all care about the morrow. For some days I have been asking the Lord that I might not look for help to any save Himself and I was especially asking Him this morning to *remember our need.* Half an hour after, a letter came from a brother in Christ containing five pounds.

Jan. 12. — I received this day two letters, one containing ten pounds and the other, not less welcome, with one pound from the dear saints at High Bickington, whose love has not grown cold during our long absence of seventeen years.

Feb. 10. — Another gift of a sovereign came from a dear brother who was one of the first converts at High Bickington.

Jan. 19. — Our poor sister Mary Marks is now living up stairs, unable to lie down, and evidently drawing near the grave. Through the abounding mercy of the Lord we are enabled to sustain the inconvenience, though the health of my dear children is little equal to it. But the Lord *has* helped and *will* help us.

Jan. 27. — A very remarkable instance of the Lord's providential care has just occurred. I was last night observing to my dear children that we had used a ton of coal in an unusually short space of time, the weather being so intensely cold, and our poor sister, to whose heart complaint dropsy is now added, was unable to lie down, and needed fire by night and day. While I was thinking about the coal this morning the post brought me a letter from Mr. M—— in which he writes as follows "I am a collier and have plenty of coals at command, and shall only be too well pleased to send you a few tons this winter. If you will allow me this gratification be kind enough to let me know how many tons you can stow away." This kind and most unexpected offer was from a gentleman whom I accidentally met at the house of a friend about six months ago, but with whom I never had any correspondence till about a week since nor did I ever recollect his name, or know that he was a proprietor of coal fields. Within a few days five tons of coal were sent me by his agent.

Jan. 30. — Our poor sister, whose mind was kept in perfect peace, departed yesterday to be with Christ. We have had the consolation of being instrumental to His comfort of this suffering child more than four years, the Lord supplying all we needed for her use without seeking help from any but Himself.

Feb. 5. — While taking my usual walk this afternoon, I asked the Lord to enable me to meet an expense which I could not well avoid, and which was likely to exceed by two or three pounds the amount I

> **SCRIPTURE TESTIMONY**
>
> *God will provide for our daily needs*
>
> MATTHEW 6:11

> **SCRIPTURE TESTIMONY**
>
> *God answers prayer*
>
> LUKE 18:7 · JOHN 15:7 · ACTS 12:5 · JAMES 5:15
>
> *God provides exactly what is needed*
>
> 2 CORINTHIANS 8:15 · PHILIPPIANS 4:19

had previously expected, and I was by the result especially reminded of the promise "Before they call I will answer, and while they are yet speaking I will hear." Isaiah 65:24. On returning home I entered through the garden and was taking off my great coat, when a knock at the front door led me to open it. A dear brother in the Lord was *there, who had brought me three sovereigns, with which he was coming to my house while I was* in prayer for that amount. It seemed also as if he thought this was his only business, as he did not come into the house, though it was perhaps the first time he had omitted to do so.

April 5. — After spending the Lord's day at T——, I was about to leave with just money enough to pay the turnpike, when the friend at whose house I was tarrying put into my hand five pounds.

May 15. — While in bed this morning, and in prospect of a long journey for which my means were not ample, I was led almost inadvertently to say "The Lord will supply all my need," and at the *same moment* I heard the postman's knock, and a letter was brought me containing ten pounds.

Aug. 5. — I am made to feel more and more my need of habitual dependence on the Lord. For some time our supplies have been small, and we began to be straitened. Just at this time two pounds were sent me by a brother in the Lord, one of which was needed for a ton of coal. When this was almost exhausted a sister sent us five shillings. Yesterday was a day of trial, but in the evening a sovereign was sent me by a brother from whom I had never heard but once before until now. May the Lord increase our faith.

Aug. 7. — Again I have to record the Lord's mercies. On Monday we felt it necessary to decline an invitation to spend the day with some Christian friends who are residing on the hill, as the small expense of turnpike was too much for us, not having even sixpence to spare until the evening, when help came. But more was soon needed, and for this we *waited and prayed*. When we thought the post must have passed, the word came to one of my dear children "Though the vision tarry, wait for it," and just after we received a letter containing ten pounds.

Feb. 14. — Our supplies of late have been very short; on my observing this last evening to my dear children one of them said, "Then we must go to our God." This morning two pounds were sent us through an entirely new channel from some unknown friend. (When this was nearly exhausted and only *fourpence* remained, ten pounds were sent us by our Heavenly Father through one of His dear servants.)

(I omitted to state that previous to my third exchange of residence, I received one morning by post, bills amounting to twenty pounds from a brother in the Lord who had heard of my intended removal. It was stated to be for this especial purpose. I have already mentioned that previous to my leaving High Bickington when the distance was *twenty* miles *five* pounds were sent to me. On the second occasion when I removed *sixty* miles *ten* pounds were sent me by one individual, and other help afterwards, and now when the distance was nearly a *hundred* miles *twenty* pounds were forwarded, which last sum was from a Christian brother whom I had not known one month previous to this time. How plainly is the hand of the Lord to be seen in such events as these, while they abundantly prove His watchful care over those who trust in the *living God.)*

Aug. 18, 1857. — My "Recollections," were completed a few weeks ago, and I have since been waiting on the Lord for directions as to their being printed; and I felt sure that if their publication would be for His glory, He would provide the means. Two days ago I received a letter from a Christian friend who has seen part of the manuscript, offering to advance the money for printing one thousand copies, adding, "I believe the impression on my mind to lend the money is of the Lord, *for I cannot get rid of the thought,* and its being paid just at this time,, after it has been out several years, seems to confirm it. I sincerely hope the Lord may greatly bless it, if He permits it to come out."

೧

J. GRIBBLE, Lower Clapton, LONDON. (N. E.)

SCRIPTURE TESTIMONY INDEX

Mr. Gribble felt led "by an agency [he] could not resist" to preach in neighboring villages and towns. Even though Mr. Gribble was truly a layman, and at a time when it was considered indispensable for a minister to have specialized training, his ministry proved to be under God's blessing, bearing much fruit for the Kingdom.

Poor old George was a blind and almost deaf fellow who having received Christ into his life gave sacrificially—and without fail—from his meagre income to support the work of God. His earthly disabilities only created a longing for heaven where he will be truly free to worship His savior.

A young man who was naturally gifted in eloquent prayer became proud and conceited. He was simply unconverted and unaware of it. Having no foundation, he was eventually led astray by the world. But through the preaching of God's Word, the young man was brought to his Savior.

A poor waggoner was returning home from work one evening when it was laid on his heart to pray—while yet an unbeliever—for his salvation. That same evening, he heard and gladly received the gospel.

After giving excuses—much like the ones first century ruler Felix gave to the Apostle Paul—a shoemaker finally attended a meeting where he listened to the message of the gospel and was deeply affected. He surrendered his life to Christ and became a new creature, able to persevere through trials.

A believing friend of Mr. Gribble had recently begun work on a fellow believer's farm. He was adamant that he would hold a weekly prayer meeting at his cottage. Given that the friend and his employer were the only believers in the region, the man was told no one would attend his prayer meeting to which he responded "then I will hold one by myself." The meetings were well attended and became a fruitful meeting place full of new believers.

Mr. Gribble's friend, having begun with hosting a prayer meeting in his cottage—alone if necessary—saw the Lord's purpose. The prayer meeting began a cascade of conversions, which led to building a small chapel, which soon became too small for the growing congregation. The result being that the whole character of the village was changed.

Believers are light in the Lord

2 Corinthians 4:6 · Ephesians 5:8

The righteous innately have God's heart toward those in need..38

Matthew 25:31-46

Gracey was a teacher from a neighboring village who had grown tired of empty novels and began to read the Bible herself, through which she came to know Christ. She then used her skills to teach a Sunday school to the effect that some of the children were moved to serve a worldly, grumpy woman in town who was sick. Gracey's humble work and teaching led the children to live out and share the Gospel in their village.

God lifts up the weak, works through them, thereby shaming the strong..43

1 Corinthians 1:27 · 1 Thessalonians 5:14

A young man of humble origins attended Mr. Gribble's meetings and fell in love with Christ. He was uneducated, unable to pray at the meetings, and persecuted for his belief at home, but God raised him up and used him for great works as a missionary.

The sheep know and hear His voice................................78

John 10:3-4 · John 10:16

While dressing one day, Robert Gribble felt deeply compelled to go preach at a village called Chittlehamholt that evening. Obeying this impulse, he set out with the help of one who knew the place and on arriving found a great reception to the message of salvation he brought.

Salvation transforms..84

2 Corinthians 5:16-17 · Galatians 6:15

Once known for her carefulness, and trouble about many worldly things like Martha in the Bible, a mother of two who finds the Lord becomes a new creature. And in place of her former character was a newfound generous hospitality.

When the wife and children of a hardhearted man surrendered their lives to Jesus, the man became a violent persecutor of their newfound faith. He often beat his wife and children and, at one point, assailed Robert Gribble for their commitment to the Gospel.

A man who came to mock the the gathering of believers was convicted by the Holy Spirit. He joined the believers the next day with his personal confession of Christ.

Robert Gribble in invited to share the Gospel at a woman's home in an unbelieving neighborhood. Forty people were there on a stormy night eager to hear the good news. The woman who invited Robert to her home became the first to accept the Christ that evening.

On the day Anne was baptized, George, her unbelieving husband was filled with rage and said many hurtful things to her. Anne, full of faith, did not retaliate but instead asked God that he be converted within a week. The next day, her husband came to her with the intent of killing her. She wept and told him she wept because of the hardness of his heart. He too began to weep, his heart softened, and he gave his life to Christ that day.

A man was at the end of his life, but he had not yet given his life to Christ because he thought his sin was too great to be forgiven. Through conversation with Robert Gribble, the man came to the understanding that Christ forgave completely, and he was reconciled to Christ. He passed away peacefully a few weeks later.

Love and honor one another in brotherly affection............ 133
Romans 12:10

Robert Gribble writes about the harmony and brotherly love that existed between him and his poor neighbor, John M. Since both men were believers in God, not only did they show each other kindness and live in peace, they were able to be a team that brought blessing to others.

Give and it shall be given unto you.............................. 134
Luke 6:38

John M. was moved to give to those in need, and gave freely, trusting the Lord to take care of his own needs. He then experienced the Lord's immediate provision, more than replacing what was given.

Communities of new believers formed by the Gospel........ 137
Acts 2:42-47

After much mental struggle, a worldly man surrendered to Christ, eventually becoming a preacher. This was the result of his sister's tireless confidence in God. She had been the only Christian in the whole community for a period. But God blessed her prayers and eventually, starting with her brother, more than one hundred fifty people came to Christ.

Holy Spirit directs believers in ministry.......................... 139
Matthew 10:19-20 · Acts 8:29 · Acts 13:2 · Acts 15:28 ·
Acts 16:6-10 · Acts 20:22 · Romans 8:14

Robert Gribble felt the leading of the Spirit to move to another village. He obeyed and was led to a village that had a great need for the gospel. By the end of his seven years' stay, he had introduced the gospel to five different places and between eighty to hundred people had converted.

Four individuals fiercely opposed the preaching of the Gospel and committed themselves to hindering its progress in their community. They did so until each one of them died an unfortunate death.

Robert Gribble was directed by the Lord to join a friend on a preaching tour, leaving his wife and children without any money. He obeyed, and his Heavenly Father took care of his family in his absence.

Robert Gribble sacrificially gives his last halfpenny to a beggar who came to beg for bread one morning. On another occasion he sends provisions to a brother in need. On both occasions, he was blessed to receive more than he had given.

A very discouraged Mr. Gribble was comforted by the timely recital of scriptures by his children at breakfast, as well as the scripture reading and hymn for that morning. These turned what seemed to be his most trying moment, into a most happy one.

After his wife's death, every single expense to be incurred as a result of her funeral was provided for. Robert Gribble placed his trust in the Lord and his needs were met by people he did not know and had never met.

Without Mr. Gribble asking, God provided the money he needed to pay his way home through a generous brother.

An unusually cold winter had caused the Gribbles to exhaust their supply of coal in a shorter than usual time. But as the father pondered his family's need, he received a letter from a brother he accidentally met six months earlier, and with whom he had never corresponded. This brother's letter was God's timely provision in their hour of need.

Robert Gribble was blessed to have the scripture, "Before they call I will answer, and while they are yet speaking I will hear," come to pass in his life when the Lord met a need while he was actively praying.

Walking Together Press is a non-profit
publishing company devoted to supporting
grassroots libraries in Africa through global book
sales and through providing free library editions.

To read our story, to see our catalog, and to learn
more about how you can help us in our mission,
visit our website at:

https://walkingtogether.press